HIMPRESSIONS

**THE BLACKWOMAN'S
GUIDE TO PAMPERING
THE BLACKMAN**

To Teresa,
From Larry —
In school we learn a lesson
and then we take a test. In life it's
just the opposite: We get tested and
then we learn the lesson.

Enjoy!
Valarie Shaw
1/18/97

HIMPRESSIONS

THE BLACKWOMAN'S
GUIDE TO PAMPERING
THE BLACKMAN

VALERIE SHAW

HarperCollins*Publishers*

HarperCollins books may be purchased for educational, business, or sales promotional use. For information please write: Special Markets Department, HarperCollins Publishers, Inc., 10 East 53rd Street, New York, NY 10022.

FIRST EDITION

Designed by Alma Hochhauser Orenstein

Library of Congress Cataloging-in-Publication Data

Shaw, Valerie,
    Himpressions : the Blackwoman's guide to pampering the Blackman / Valerie Shaw. — 1st ed.
        p.   cm.
    ISBN 0-06-017435-8
    1. Afro-American men. 2. Afro-American women.   I. Title.
E185.86.S56   1996
305.3'089'96073—dc20   96-3844

96 97 98 99 00 ❖/RRD 10 9 8 7 6 5 4 3 2 1

For Andrew, Mother, Hoppie, "Doc" Smith, Andrea,
and other angels I have known

Pleasant words are as a honeycomb, sweet to the soul, and health to the bones.

PROVERBS 16:24

The tongue is a little member, and boasts great things. Behold, how great a matter a little fire kindleth!

JAMES 3:5

Who can find a virtuous woman? For her price is far above rubies.

PROVERBS 31:10

CONTENTS

PREFACE

She who runs from the red ant may stumble upon the stinging ant.

ETHIOPIAN PROVERB

God must have a great sense of humor. Why else would he make me the mother of a Black man-child? You see, throughout my life, I can trace most of my problems to Black men. Up until the birth of my son, in fact, I ran from relationships with men—Blackmen in particular—at warp speed.

My parents split up when I was twelve. I wasn't abused or neglected, but when our dad moved to a different city, remarried a White woman, and began a new family, my sister and I were devastated.

I've been married three times. My first marriage, right out of college and right out of *Modern Bride* magazine, ended after we'd both been unfaithful.

Emerging from a five-year hiatus, I remarried—with the vow that I'd do everything to make it work. After eight years, my husband told me that I'd done too much. He was leaving.

My third marriage—well, that's a chapter that is still being written. Let me just say that if it hadn't been for the beautiful son we brought into the world, I'm sure that we would have only been passing boats in the bay. For years, our baby boy was the only thing we had in common.

I didn't hate men; I just didn't understand them, and I was growing to fear them, becoming man-shy because of so many bad experiences.

Giving birth to my son was the crisis that brought me face to face with my fears. For in spite of my trepidations, in spite of my apprehensions, and in spite of my efforts to avoid Blackmen, I was now required to mother one.

My son, now ten years old, is my first test subject in pampering the Blackman, for it is my goal to raise a son who will grow up to be a good man, a caring husband, and a loving father.

His father, too, has been a great guide. Having been married for twelve years—and having had more separations than Elizabeth Taylor and Richard Burton—we are dedicated to staying friends, regardless of where our relationship takes us.

I believe that it was my destiny to write *Himpressions: The Blackwoman's Guide to Pampering the Blackman*. Besides sharing my birthday, October 16, with the Million Man March, I am like the manicurist who used to bite her fingernails or the hairstylist who once wore a wig. Because of my own outlandish experiences, I am empathically dedicated to the preservation of Black relationships.

ACKNOWLEDGMENTS

Mother tells me that I burst from her womb with a rush—as though I were racing to get someplace. I've been running ever since.

Thanks to the Creator, whom I call God, for including me in his divine plan and for supreme direction throughout all of my stumbling, bungling, and most unsure steps.

Thanks to my family—my mother, Earline Shaw Johnson; my two dads, Bennie Shaw and Bill Johnson; my son, Andrew Amy, and my tremendous step-family—the whole Amy clan of sons and daughters; all the Shaw siblings—in particular, my sister Benita; and Candece Wilson, my adopted daughter—all of whom love me as though I was always a winner, even when I come in dead last.

Others who bet on me before my ambition left the gate and to whom I am eternally grateful are my Sister-cousins Dwan Smith-Fortier and Sandera Shaw; my spiritual Sisters Sharon Givens, Joanna Johnson, Rachel Martinez, Frances Nealy, Gail Saunders, Jonnie Summers, Mary Margaret Swift, and Kay White; and the finest protégé a mentor ever had, Andrea James.

To the teachers, coaches, mentors, and sages who were angels in my life and have since made their transition: Emma Hartman and Mary McCoo (my other mothers), Mrs. Mueller, Mrs. Shirley, Harry Tolliver, Sandy Simon, Thomas Lakin, Kenneth

Owler Smith, and Russell Caldwell; and to subsequent wise ones who smoothed the rough edges and always had an encouraging word for my ideas: David Crowther, Robert Epstein, Bill Faith, Joe Saltzman, and Jerry Whelan.

To Khalifa Abdur-Raheem, the first spiritual mentor and guide to assist me down my path, and to Rev. Charles Rose, who fills me with inspiration every Sunday, I humbly thank you.

For those who embraced me as a true shoe-repair lady—Jack Lynch, the late Alex B. Thomas, and Henry Feltenberg—and for those who flung open the gates to Hollywood without question, embracing me as the "First Lady of Soles"—Bill Welsh, Johnny Grant, John Adams and the Hollywood Chamber of Commerce, Rick Dees, and Earl Lestz, may this book speak volumes to your kindness.

To all of the master cobblers and shine men—my "cowboys"—who helped me understand the Blackman's pain and inspired me to do something about it, this work is for you.

And to the first "nice" girl I ever knew, Jo Bonita Smith, and the first "nice" guy I ever loved, John Simmons, thanks for the early models of lovingkindness.

Thanks to fellow travelers at points along the way who have greatly impacted my life and often changed its course: Bayyinah Ali, Art Amy Sr., Jacque Bee, Willie Bellamy, Paul Bozenhard, Tony Chavez, Sukari Christian, Jim Cleaver, U. C. Davis, Alvin Durand, Rita Dyson, Mike Ellison and Christine Goodreau, Bette Floyd Okanlawon, Rex Fortune, Yvonne Gillium, Al Grant, Annett Green, Al Greenstein, Kenneth Harris, Ann Jackson, David Maxwell, Milton McGriff, Bridgette Rose McNeill, Rosie Milligan, Donna Mungen, Matt Nadler, Rosita Odom, David Reeves, Emma Rodgers, Juanita Thomas, Glenn Timony, Arnold Washington, Maxine Waters, Debra Williams, and Jackie Woodard.

And for working to bring my inner beauty out of the closet, thank you to CieJai Perez, Rea Tur Ree, and Cheryl Tyus.

For demonstrating the finest qualities in Black manhood, husbandhood, parenthood, and/or sonhood—Michael Anderson,

Robert Ashley, Ben Blakley, Reginald Brass, R. L. Bryant, Ron Brewington, Larry Carroll, Rodney Conner, George Cook, Earl "Skip" Cooper III, Al DeBlanc, Dennis DeLoach, Edward Ellis, Harry Elston, Nate Fortier Jr., Alfred Green, James Harrison, Bill Hayes, Soloman Herbert, Richard Hill, Nate Holden, Emory Holmes, Robert Hopkins, Earl Ofari Hutchinson, Roland Jefferson, Clint Johnson, Steve Johnson, Bob Jones, Warren Lanier Sr., Walter Maynard Sr., Larry McCormick, Dwight McLurkin, Don Murphy, Carl Nelson, James Odom, Ekundayo Paris, Larry Payne, Gary Pérard, Leonard Reed, Elvin Ricks, Matt Shaw, Wilson Simmons, Toy Snipes, Marshall Taylor, Paul Turner (and all the jocks at KKDA-AM), Ralph Walker, Richard Whitfield, Chester Whitmore, Carl Prince Williams, Everett Williams, Michael Williams, Rickey Williams, Msuniso Usafi, and Calistro Veasey—thanks for the shining examples.

And finally, to the "A Team" who brought this author out of obscurity and put my work on track: J. T. O'Hara, (the goddess of literary networking), Paul S. Levine (the business attorney from heaven), Jim Hornfischer and Frank Weimann (agents beyond compare), Maureen O'Neal (the senior editor who stepped way out on faith of the unknown), and Trena Keating (who nurtured it to the finish line), this book is a testament to your belief in me for which I thank you with all my heart.

And to the HarperCollins support staff who polished this, my first book, like a jewel, thanks to Mary O'Shaughnessy, Joseph Montebello, Suzanne Noli, and Nancy Palmer Jones.

For making my personal race such a joy-filled adventure, thank you one and all.

FOREWORD

Folks think that being a relationship author from Los Angeles is an oxymoron. L.A. and commitment just don't go together. In a city where divorce rates are nearly double the national average, the prospects of holding on to a man are about as stable as the San Andreas fault.

I, too, as a Los Angeles native, am convinced that L.A. is one of the toughest cities in the world in which to maintain a long-term healthy relationship.

[Cutting your teeth on a relationship in Los Angeles is like taking your first flying lesson in a Stealth bomber.]

Just think, L.A. Sisters have to compete for men with the most beautiful women in the world, of all nationalities, who come to Hollywood every day by the jumbo-jet–load to seek their fame and fortune in the City of Angels.

[Now that's some serious competition.]

I have a friend who met her husband-to-be at a large midwest-ern university where they both attended law school. When he was offered a partnership in a new firm, they came west.

Girlfriend got a few offers but also got pregnant shortly after the move. One year after the twins were born, she went to work for the public defender's office.

Meanwhile, a new secretary was hired by her husband's

expanding law firm—a beautiful ebony-colored velvet-skinned doll from East Texas, whom I called the "Black Lolita."

While her husband did his business in air-conditioned splendor, Girlfriend had more jobs than a night nurse on duty in an inner-city emergency room.

At home she was Mommy to the twins and Boss Lady to the baby-sitter (who barely spoke English). At work—after a forty-five-minute commute—she was an undervalued, underpaid, and overworked public defender who, more often than not, watched her indigent clients go to jail.

The strain was too much. She was drained. She had a bad day.

[Girlfriend was certainly entitled to a bad day now and again, for goodness' sakes.]

And so she had one, again.

She felt tired. Tired and overwhelmed. Her bad days turned into bad weeks. She was too exhausted to go out. Or to make love.

Dinner became microwavable or "get it yourself."

She couldn't communicate her feelings to her husband. She didn't even know what she was feeling.

Homeboy began to stay late at the office. One night the Black Lolita was putting in a little overtime herself, to catch up on her work.

Pretty soon, Girlfriend's husband and the Black Lolita were looking like Perry Mason and Della Street, pulling down those after-hours shifts.

One night it was too late for him to drive home. So he crashed in Lo's apartment.

[It was raining, and she lived nearby, don't you know.]

I don't know the details, but I heard that the Black Lolita made breakfast. It was her grandmother's recipe for French toast.

Before you could say, "Oops, there it goes," another Black marriage in the City of Angels bit the dust.

For those Los Angeles Sisters who haven't been the victim of an unfaithful spouse, most have been conned, compromised, or scammed by one of those Big-City Boys coming to Hollywood from every metropolitan center on the globe to run a game.

[I'm telling you, Girlfriend, the race to stay in a relationship these days is as tough as the triathlon.]

It has always been a puzzle to me how, against odds that are greater than Powerball, some couples manage not only to stay together but to thrive together, even through times of great uncertainty, with temptations abounding.

I had never had an opportunity to talk to such couples until 1989, when I became the managing partner of a new high-technology shoe repair and shine salon on the world-famous corner of Sunset and Vine in Hollywood.

Soon after opening our doors to the public, I began to meet interesting men and women who defied my writer's sensibilities about Hollywood and the fragility of relationships.

Gentlemen stopped in for a shoe shine and a little conversation. And gentle ladies hurried through our doors with bags of shoes to be repaired—their heels, their husbands' boots, and their kids' tennies.

I wasn't at all surprised when our exquisite salon began to attract a lot of Hollywood high rollers—studio executives and stars who had some vanity about their appearance. I rather expected that once the word was out, our clientele, like birds following a trail of crumbs, would grow to include an assortment of men who had to think fast on their feet—lawyers, police officers, salesmen, bus drivers, and postal workers.

Soon, they were joined by a few wing-tipped bankers and stockbrokers who led double lives as weekend Texas-cowboy-boot-wearin' ranchers.

Not surprisingly, our shoe shine salon saw more male activity than the Pentagon under red alert. Business was booming!

[I'm tellin' you, the place was rockin' with Rockports and rolling in San Remos.]

One day, working the counter, I was surprised to wait on an elegant, ebony-colored, velvet-skinned thirtysomething Sister with a bag of shoes—hers, her husband's, and the kids' tennies—whom I recognized as the Black Lolita. Now, that surprised me!

I was surprised, in fact, at the significant percentage of women who quietly slipped in with their husband's shoes for repairs and shines. For the most part, they insisted that their overt gestures of thoughtfulness remain covert.

"I wouldn't tell my family because this is my second marriage and they'll say I'm copping out," said one fortyish female customer with a bag of men's shoes spilled before her on the counter.

[As they do with a barber, bartender, or cosmetologist, most folks just naturally confide in their "shine" lady.]

One Sister said she wouldn't share her secret because she didn't want to appear to be antifeminist to her girlfriends.

Several women told me they couldn't take the ribbing from coworkers if anyone caught them catering to a man.

[And the Black Lolita confided, upon picking up her order, that she wasn't about to slip up and lose out to a younger model.]

I was surprised too, in hours of listening to these New Relationship Sisters—many of whom had been married for years—that I was beginning to employ some of their tactics in my own ongoing skirmishes with Brothers. And I was certainly surprised when these new strategies began to work.

Bragging to some young Sisters one day about my new and improved attitude toward relationships, I was challenged to appear on *The Love Connection* by some of my "cowboys" and male customers who had been eavesdropping on the conversation.

Before my days as a Hollywood shoe shine lady, I could never have envisioned myself pampering a "love connection" to perfection on nationally syndicated television. But after that first public declaration of where I stood on the issue of pampering the Blackman, there was no turning back.

The shoe business was dissolved in 1993, and I've changed my course from saving soles to saving souls, now that I have witnessed the true power of Pampership.

I've spent the last five years interviewing over one thousand men and women in ongoing research, defending my position on television and radio talk shows and to incredulous Sisters who don't believe that something so simple could work so well.

[Girlfriend, you'll never be able to convince me that pampering doesn't make life easier. Today I am more than a proponent of pampering; I am a disciple.]

And I don't think that it is such a coincidence that over the last few years, my relationships with family, friends, and significant others have been relatively fight free.

Now, at age fifty-one, it is my great and humble pleasure to share the experiences and conversations—gathered from a Hollywood shoe shine parlor and beyond—that convince me that Sisters today have the untapped and overlooked power to change the destiny of their relationships through the nurturing arts.

And it seems to me that if we can change the destiny of our relationships, we can change the course of history. Maybe that's what my mother meant, forty years ago, when she told me, "The hand that rocks the cradle rules the world." Thanks, Mom; now I get it!

DEDICATION

To men, all men,
Your passion's deep,
If only passion's not put to sleep.
To women, my Sisters,
Who know not their power,
This is the time,
Now is the hour.
Heal the wounds
Of a past out of control,
Today, the present, is ours to hold.
Oh, mothers, daughters,
Sisters, wives, and friends,
Let go the anger,
Let us celebrate our men.

VALERIE SHAW

HIMPRESSIONS

THE BLACKWOMAN'S
GUIDE TO PAMPERING
THE BLACKMAN

INTRODUCTION

1

If you are concerned about the effect your presence has on others, you care about the impression you are making.

There are first impressions, lasting impressions, good impressions, and wrong impressions. But those, it seems to me, fall short of describing the impressions we have about (and try to leave with) the opposite sex.

Women, in particular, are concerned about the impression they make on men. Did I say concerned? I mean *consumed*.

It is no secret that men are our favorite topic of conversation at work, over lunch, on the telephone, and behind their backs. It is amazing how much time we spend dissecting a male's behavior and peccadilloes.

From the books we read to the shows we watch, from where we go to what we wear, men are our oxygen.

For every one man's action there is a shower of female reaction. We always have something to say. Or to add.

A date that took three hours to enjoy takes six hours to pick apart. After describing the event in more detail than CNN covering the O. J. Simpson double-murder trial, you ask your girlfriend, "Does it sound like he likes me?"

As if she'd occupied the press box in the backseat of his car, you press on. "Do you think he'll ask me out again?"

If she is a truly wise friend, she'll admit that she doesn't know. But that's not what you want to hear. That's not why you called her! Girlfriend is supposed to wrap up your story, like Oprah, and lead the audience in applause.

[Cut to the commercial.]

You want some assurances. Hope. Some kind of guarantee that he's thinking about you as much as you're thinking about him. Even if it is a fantasy as big as *The Lion King,* you want to hear it in Dolby Stereo.

Now, things are bad between the sexes all over the world. Divorce rates are soaring among all races. Unhappiness and loneliness are epidemic. Feelings of isolation are as universal as mother's milk.

Somewhere, however, between Vietnam and O. J. Simpson— with a benchmark pit stop at the confirmation hearings for Justice Clarence Thomas—Blackwomen have been especially hard hit by shrapnel from the War Between the Sexes.

In Vietnam we lost over thirty thousand of our brightest and finest young men. That was the sixties, when life was supposed to be simple.

Then along came the seventies and eighties. Sisters lost about two generations of Brothers (or a couple of million men) to drugs, crime, and homosexuality and their deadly cousins— homicide, prison, and AIDS.

Many of us shaken into the eighties' reality of scarcity went back to school to get a degree or to advance our education. Many of us climbed the career ladder—just as we expected *him* to do.

While that was a personally satisfying trip in the eighties, doesn't it piss you off (just a teeny bit) that when you look back, in the nineties, most Brothers are nowhere to be found? Some unfortunate Sisters have even slid backward—moved back home or into the lap of Big Brother Welfare along with their growing fatherless families.

By now, in the nineties, some honest Sisters sadly admit that we are the biggest casualties of the sexual revolution of the sixties.

Most Sisters today are used to operating their lives without a man at the helm. So when we do meet the real endangered Blackman who has his act together, we are so used to being in the driver's seat that we refuse to give up the wheel.

["He don't know where he's going. Give me that steering wheel!" CRASH!!!]

The same leadership and independence that free us to be the heads of our families, our community-based organizations, our schools, and our businesses make us the butts of the Blackman's jokes.

Bossy, opinionated, stubborn, selfish—these are some of the words that keep cropping up in a Blackman's conversation about Sisters.

To older gents we are *sarcastic Sapphires* (reminiscent of *Amos 'n' Andy*'s Sapphire, the shrilling shrew married to the Kingfish).

To the boys in the hood we are *b*'s and *w*'s.

To space-age Trekkie-type Brothers with a futuristic view of the world, we are an *alien species*.

And even to many Bible-toting Blackmen, who say they try to give us a Christian chance, we are *deceitful Delilahs* who won't just give a Brother a haircut—they say we're trying to cut off their balls, too.

While she stood tall as a card-carrying heroine to most Sisters, Anita Hill simply confirmed to many Brothers that it's open season on the Blackman.

"The Sisters' Revenge," one of my male patrons once called the Clarence Thomas hearings and the Mike Tyson conviction for rape. "You'll stop at nothing to ruin us."

Men say that now not only do they face incredible obstacles on the job and in the street but we Black Sisters are taking private grievances with our men to the airwaves.

And it's true that today, the war between Brothers and Sisters is heating up over the airwaves like popcorn. The only Black relationships we're exposed to, 24-7, are the sick ones. The ones that absolutely don't work.

[For one entire year during prime time, we caught three or four hours of O. J. Simpson's trial of the millennium, live on three channels. O. J. reminded us of the Blackman's ultimate treachery—marrying a White woman.]

For a break, we tuned in a few hours of talk show terrorists' bombing attacks—with men as the stationary targets.

[If his woman is constantly firing on him, is it any wonder why a Brother would be missing in action?]

Without assigning blame, I'd just like to point out that somewhere between our own bad experiences and all the bad news bombarding us, we have bought into the stereotypes about Blackmen, and we have sold them short.

Blackwomen have fashioned for themselves a manless matriarchy, and a Brother doesn't have a chance.

[Most Sisters today have stopped breathing life into their relationships. They are merely "waiting to exhale."]

Experience has taught us that if a Brother doesn't suffer from cold feet or spinelessness, he's got a case of "jungle fever." He's going to take you for a ride, or you're going to get soaked. Before he steals your heart, you might as well cut him off at the knees.

We reserve these judgments strictly for the Blackman, I'm afraid.

You won't hear too many mothers warning their daughters about the perils of falling for a White man—Jew or Gentile. And we're altogether mute on Hispanic and Asian men. But don't we have a lot to say about our Brothers?

I began calling our radical and emotionally charged opinions about the Blackman *himpressions* after realizing that our feelings go way beyond mere *impressions.*

Our *himpressions* of our Brothers are the result of generations of estrangement.

[We haven't really spoken civilly to each other since slavery, when we had only one common oppressor.]

"He's worse than a deadbeat dad, he's a deadbeat dog."

"That lazy womanizer can't make nothin' but a baby."

". . . And he'll never amount to nothin'. That sorry SOB."

Those are a few of our *himpressions* of Blackmen in the nineties.

We forget that our men are also our sons, so the result of our negative *himpressions* is the generation-wide dysfunctional African-American family, which is as common today as family court and welfare.

Come on, Girlfriend, admit it. We *do* have a problem.

I'm a woman. A Blackwoman. But I'm also a writer who served three years on the front line in the War Between the Sexes in a shoe shine shop.

I guess you could say that I formed an economic alliance with the enemy—men. Working in a male-dominated business, over half of my customers and all of my "cowboys" (that's what I called my master cobblers and shine personnel) were men.

From what I heard and overheard—from hundreds of men and from the cowboys—is that Brothers are frustrated with Sisters in a major way.

"That nagging bitch makes me want to stay in the streets," said one hardworking, self-employed single father about his live-in lover.

"She can criticize me all day long," a young accountant told his friend, "but the minute I check her on something, she's ready to call the police."

"Just tell her I'm not here," said one of the cowboys when he got a phone call. "That woman must not have anything to do except bug me once *Geraldo* is over," he muttered.

I wondered, how many times had I been dissed in a juicy barbershop or shoe shine parlor conversation?

[Oh, well—other men, other times.]

The frustration with Sisters seems to be a common thread that runs through the very fabric of the Brotherhood. To them we are all alike.

Now where have I heard *that* one before?

I was sincerely amazed at all the years I had wasted on trying to understand the Blackman. With all the time my girlfriends and I have dedicated to dissecting the African-American male psyche we could have retired the national debt or discovered the cure for AIDS.

So much time. So much wasted time. So much energy. So much wasted energy!

"So *stop,*" I said to myself after eavesdropping on one particularly frank all-male conversation. "Stop trying to figure out what a Blackman thinks. Ask him."

I discovered that Brothers are almost always willing to talk about their feelings, their preferences, what makes them happy, and what gets on their last nerve.

Most of the men I talked to wondered why it had taken us so long to ask.

It occurred to me that if we understood Brothers and changed some of our *himpressions,* we could save ourselves a lot of needless grief, and we could help to create healthy relationships between Black men and women in the process.

So what do we do with this understanding?

"I'm just looking for a woman who will pamper me," said one of my very handsome bachelor friends several years ago.

PAMPER?!

What an interesting choice of words.

Pamper, as in coddle? Overindulge? Give in to? Kiss up to?

Pamper. An old notion that must have come out of the charcoal ages of the antebellum South.

Pamper. That's what the man said.

I had to think about that one for a moment.

You pamper a baby or a household pet, don't you? You also pamper the people you love.

With an abused puppy or a neglected child, you must necessarily give a little more love, a little more understanding, and a lot of compassion to make the relationship work. The time and effort you expend is—in a word—*pampering.*

Well, by everyone's acknowledgment—social scientists, the media, the clergy, and the bookie on the corner—the Blackman is both neglected and abused.

And if that's not enough, the Blackman in the 1990s is the most endangered species walking on two legs on the North American continent.

I recall a study I read in the *New England Journal of Medicine* that said a Blackman in Harlem was less likely to live to the age of sixty-five than a man in Bangladesh, one of the world's poorest nations.

[Girlfriend, you know that's a shame.]

Hm-m-m, abused, neglected, and endangered. It sounds to me like Brothers deserve some pampering.

Today, as we measure our lives in nanoseconds, survival issues pressing in like ants on watermelon, pampering takes on new meaning.

In the past five years, I've asked thousands of men to comment on the notion of pampering. Early into my informal investigation, one pampered Blackman I know described his soulmate as a woman who provided a refuge from his stress.

"She *knows* how to pamper me, man," he said with a quarter-moon grin lighting his face. "My lady makes me smile, keeps me laughing, and reminds me every day that she's in my corner."

"I'd feel pampered if I could find a woman who wanted to help me make some money instead of plotting to take my money," said one of my bachelor customers.

"All she needs to do is rub my back and keep my feet warm," quipped another.

The word *pamper* raised a torrent of response, breaking through the wall of silence between me and the men in my salon like a shout of SOS on the open seas.

In most cases, among the less verbose Brothers, pampering meant just being nice. Kind. Understanding. A woman who wouldn't take them for an emotion-filled ride on a runaway train headed straight for the brick-wall side of the poorhouse.

Pampering a man was just that simple.

And that was the genesis for this guide.

As a social scientist, I've got to tell you that developing a model of understanding between hassled Brothers and hostile Sisters was a great research challenge.

[It might be easier to stop a genocide on foreign soil.]

But amazingly, in the twenty-four months I spent compiling

and testing my original *himpressions* and theories about pampering, I discovered more fine, eligible Brothers hungry for meaningful relationships than I had in the previous twenty-four years.

Brothers were everywhere! Suddenly I was holding seven winning numbers in the Lottery of Love.

So here I am, three marriages, several engagements, and an ocean of heartache later, enjoying new waves of Brothers washing onto my shores.

I've met dozens of other Sisters who—regardless of age, looks, and social status—have also found an abundance of manna in the wasteland. These are Sisters who have more dates than a homemade fruitcake.

Their secret?

Well, that's what *Himpressions* is about.

Please don't tell me there are no good Blackmen. That's like saying there is no fruit on the old apple tree.

I am convinced that many Sisters are either picking from the wrong orchard or trying to harvest a crop out of season.

[Whatever.]

I just think that it's time for Sisters to dig in and take the initiative in harvesting a bumper crop of men. Today, in the nineties, isn't it time to replant our relationships in fertile soil?

Admittedly, my *himpressions* are not for everyone. If you are looking for something high tech or high-sounding, you are definitely turning the wrong page. There is absolutely nothing complex about this guide.

Himpressions: The Blackwoman's Guide to Pampering the Blackman is a recipe book of "beauty shop" secrets that may help my Sisters to serve our starving Brotherhood a slice of fresh, warm apple pie in the waning years of this millennium.

As far as relationship books go, I like to think of this one as a tray of desserts.

You might want to call it a *pamper sampler.*

Now, let's get busy!

2   HIMPRESSIONS: WHERE THEY COME FROM

To my late maternal grandmother—growing up in the rural Jim Crow South, assaulted by field bosses and field-workers, and abused by the men who came courting and the men she married—all men were dogs.

That's the sermon she preached to her dying day.

Of all my relatives, on both sides of the family, and of all my friends, I can count only a handful of *successfully* married couples. Successful, as in working together for common goals and truly caring for each other's well-being.

Most Black folks I know are in dysfunctional relationships. Or abusive relationships.

[Is "abuse" dysfunctional enough for you?]

Aside from the clinically dysfunctional, many a Sister is the primary breadwinner, chief caregiver, and sole decision maker in her family. Wearing so many hats, a Sister may consider it a part of her job to keep her spouse in his place—somewhere behind her, along with the kids.

[After all, she's the one doing the moving and the shaking. Everyone else is just baggage. Or along for the ride.]

*   *   *

Don't you wonder where we get our *himpressions* about Blackmen?

From our grandmothers, half of whom raised their children (our mothers and fathers) without a man; or from our mothers, two-thirds of whom became jaundiced by abandonment, loneliness, and nonpayment of child support?

Or do we get these one-dimensional *himpressions* about Brothers from our friends, who are, more often than not, single or divorced, bitter and alone?

From the movies? Television? Music videos? Maybe from *Lifestyles of the Rich and Famous*? *Russell Simmon's Def Comedy Jam*? *Martin*? or *Living Single*? The soap operas? Talk shows? Or ads in *Ebony Man*?

The answer, sadly, is all of the above. Most of our information about men comes to us secondhand, from hearsay or from the media.

[Whatever way it arrives on your doorstep, my Sister, you'd best believe that it's scripted by someone else.]

Most Sisters out there in the male marketplace were raised by single mothers. What are those statistics? I've read that 68 percent of all Black households are headed by women.

Personally I don't know of more than a couple dozen households that aren't now or haven't been, for long stretches of time, headed by women.

I wonder how we can form a healthy respect for men when most Sisters don't even know the opposite sex. Most of us Sisters were raised by our mothers!

So where was your father during your formative years?

My dad was in a new marriage, raising another family, completely uninvolved in my sister's and my upbringing.

Some fathers were deceased. Others were in jail or in the military. Same thing. They were gone!

Even those of us who shared our growing up with brothers were, more often than not, estranged from our male siblings. While our brothers practiced their manhood thing—identifying with absent fathers or ever-present friends—sisters were rarely brought into the inner circle. Our observations about men were developed at the dinner table or from fights over use of the bathroom.

I don't know too many adult Black siblings—brothers and sisters—who are close. In fact, I don't know too many Black men and women, of any relation, who are good friends.

It's a strange war we're waging against each other. Both Sisters and Brothers admit that we share the same struggle to survive in these troubling times.

We don't have a problem admitting, anyway, that we do need each other on many fronts.

Take the money thing. Rent (or that hefty mortgage), car payments and maintenance, the ever-rising cost of living and double-digit inflation. The truth is, two do live cheaper than one.

And today with AIDS overtaking African-Americans by two to one in comparison with the general population—these days, two also live *healthier* than one.

Ask the opposing sides: both armies say they want peace. Both the Brothers and the Sisters say they want to come together.

I hear it every day:

"Girl, can't you introduce me to a good man?" one Sister begs her friend.

"When I do," says her friend, "he'll be my husband."

From the other side of the war zone I hear, "Man, I'd be married tomorrow if I could find a woman who wanted more from me than help with rent and baby-sitting."

The blame, says each side, rests squarely with that *other* gender.

Girlfriend says, "You know, there just aren't any good men left who aren't married."

Homeboy, on the other hand, declares, "Man, I'd give anything to meet a woman who isn't a man-eater."

Meanwhile the "personals" are bulging. The bars are bursting. And E-mail is exploding.

Everybody's looking for somebody.

A Brother will spend two hundred dollars for a night of champagne and cruisin' and the next morning have nothing more than a headache, some empty bottles, and one spent condom between the sheets.

A Sister will spend two hours primping for a date she really doesn't want to go on and then spend the night with this stranger who could be wanted in three states.

Both the Brothers and the Sisters are looking for the best but fully expecting to find the worst.

Low expectations bring poor results.

Many of my Sisters get just what they expect.

It seems to me that the Blackwoman's struggle to meet and keep the endangered Blackman in her pocket is like going to Las Vegas with an empty purse and bad credit.

With no money, she can't even play the slot machines.

And if you can't play, you sure can't win.

[What's happening?]

Building positive relationships out of negative perceptions is a lot like building sand castles at the beach. Oh, what a big wave'll do to a fragile sand castle.

Now, if our old *himpressions* aren't working, why don't we form some new ones? Maybe by changing our perceptions and *himpressions* about the Blackman we can bring about a positive change in our relationships with him.

Let me warn you, though, my Sister. By throwing out all of your tired old *himpressions* about the Blackman and making up your mind to build healthy new ones, you will, at first, recognize a tremendous void in your conversations with your girlfriends.

Suddenly, without anything negative to say, you'll have nothing to talk about.

But if your goal is to build positive, lasting relationships with our Brothers, I promise you that unless you abandon that old mine shaft of past hurts and rejections, you'll never strike gold.

Just look at it this way: it's impossible to strike gold in a deserted shaft. It's already been worked over.

Let's start fresh as squeezed orange juice.

Throw out those tired old experiences with the evening trash and start anew.

For goodness' sakes—and for your happiness' sake—don't take my word on it. I invite you to form some *himpressions* of your own.

3 INSECURITY: THE BLACK PLAGUE OF RELATIONSHIPS

The way I see it, the black plague of our species is *insecurity*. In order for you to appreciate a wonderful man in your life, you've got to learn to appreciate yourself first!

So the first step in pampering your man is really learning to pamper yourself. That means shedding the winter coat of insecurity and walking, bikini-confident, into the sunshine.

Don't even think that you can't do it!

If I could, anyone can.

For most of my life I've felt like an outsider—an uninvited guest at Christmas dinner, a dwarf playing guard in the NBA, a pimply faced pubescent modeling on a Paris runway.

I can still recall the horrors of my teenage years. When I danced with a boy, I had sweaty palms, knocking knees, and my body gave off that funky smell of fear and imminent danger.

Needless to say, I didn't dance much. But to compensate, I learned to talk. And talk. And talk.

That, I was good at.

They say that women generally talk too much.

I recall one guy I had set my sights on telling me that I'd be great if I didn't try so hard to be great.

I had no idea what he meant. I just kept on talking. I could be counted on, in those days, to monopolize any conversation.

[Why, I could have taken the gold medal in the Talk Olympics.]

But then, that was before I got into the shoe shine business and learned, for the first time in my life, to listen.

Believe it or not, more progressive men over the age of twenty-nine get their shoes shined than step into any locker room.

Just ask a Brother. A successful man knows that his appearance counts from head to toe. It's a grooming thing.

See, the shoe shine parlor is the male equivalent of the female beauty shop. Just like we do when we get a scalp massage during a shampoo, men getting their feet worked on feel relaxed. And comfortable.

And they talk, just like Sisters. Oh, do they love to talk!

At work in the shine salon, I often felt as though I was eavesdropping on a party line. Or listening at the bedroom door of a bachelor party.

Needless to say, I had more fun on my job than a pig in a garbage dump or a fox in the henhouse. In three years in the shoe biz, I heard more secret yearnings and confessions from Brothers than Dear Abby.

"That's interesting," I observed one day several years ago. "I'm learning more about men by listening than I ever did by talking."

Now that I think about it, most people—women especially—talk incessantly out of insecurity. We're uncomfortable with silence, or we want to impress a man with how many virtues we possess.

God, if we leave something out he won't recognize how sensitive and intelligent we are. Better get it all in—in one breath!

"... And so after I graduated from Stanford I was a social worker in the inner city before I joined the bank and bought an expensive condo in Hillsboro. But then, when my mother got sick and I had to take time off work and go back to Cleveland ..."

Have you ever noticed at the end of an evening how much of your life's tragedy you've shared but how little you know about him?

He might know your net worth, and you don't even know his phone number.

So you want to be different in his eyes? Well, surprise, my Sister, if you're talking enough to get dry mouth, you fit his stereotype. You are as common as a potato in a sack. As soon as a Brother has peeled you, you are nothing more than a French fry. Or worse, you're mashed.

If you want to stay out of the skillet, Girlfriend, try listening. It's as easy as that.

Once you warm up to the idea of listening, you'll be amazed at how your own insecurity will dissipate.

You are not alone on this planet. Lots of people feel the same way you do. They face fears, challenges, disappointments, just like you do. The more you begin to experience empathy for other people, the less insecure you will feel within yourself.

The good habit of listening leads to learning—about yourself, about him, about other points of view.

And with two of every three Black marriages ending in divorce these days, I think it's time for someone to start doing some listening.

If talking too much or listening too little is not the problem, many Sisters are driven deep into the clutches of insecurity by an abusive mate.

If you're being used as a doormat, pillow, or punching bag, it is no wonder that you feel like you're worth less than the furniture.

If you are so mauled that you can't get a grip on your own survival and you can't live without the pain, of course you are too insecure to beat a path to the door.

But in far too many cases, Sisters *choose* to stay in an unhappy relationship. More than that, they stretch it out.

"What did I do wrong?"

"What can I do to make him love me"—or "to get him back?"

"What will I do with the rest of my life without him?"

On New Year's Eve, 1970, as I sat by the Santa Monica shore contemplating suicide because of a broken engagement and a broken heart, I asked myself that question a thousand times.

I shall never forget that darkest night, praying for a way to die or for a reason to live.

Of those hours of great anguish I can remember only three words that seemed to well up inside of me like the pounding surf. They came from an inner voice that spoke plainly and distinctly: *"He's not it."*

I interpreted the message to mean that my former fiancé was neither my excuse for dying nor my reason for living. So, too timid to make any positive decision, I simply alternated between chasing him (to make him change his mind) and hibernating (from the rest of the world) for three more years after our inevitable and final breakup.

I lost another two years in pining away over the breakup of my second marriage.

Five years of my life were lost to the feeling that I could not live without a man to love me.

One thing I think Brothers learn in sports but Sisters don't learn anywhere is that getting dumped is not personal.

In every contest—as in sports, as in the military, in business, and the War Between the Sexes—there is a winner and there is a loser. A dumper and a dumpee. It's not personal. Someone's just got to bite the dust.

Looking at it that way, Girlfriend, if you spend all your time mourning lost loves, I guarantee that you'll feel sorry for yourself. And self-pity is the lifeblood of *insecurity.*

Self-pity will blind you to your potential and overshadow all of your accomplishments. It will rob you of the pleasure of all future relationships. And you'll be far too busy feeling sorry for yourself today to build a more promising tomorrow.

[In moments when I begin to feel self-pity, I remind myself that life is not a hotel. You can't just lie there and expect to be served. You've got to get up.]

Getting up means moving. And as you move through life, the scenery changes.

I mean, if the only people you know now are the same people you've always known, you won't have any room to meet the people you haven't met yet.

Right?

Your best friend in the first grade is probably not your best friend today. Different times bring different folks into your life.

There! I rest my case.

OK, so developing a strong sense of self-esteem isn't as easy as cracking open an egg.

The good feelings we have about ourselves are often buried beneath layers of social and personal heartache, rejection, and neglect. But they *are* there.

Every now and then—when you get your hair done in a sexy new style, lose weight, get an unexpected compliment from your boss, or even make one positive decision—you feel a rush of self-esteem.

[I like to look at the change in a woman who goes in for an acrylic fingernail job. She goes in like a hausfrau and comes out like Her Highness. Her grace is all a matter of self-perception.]

The rush of self-esteem reminds you of all the self-confidence that is your potential. For just a moment you are Queen of the Universe.

Now, what if you hadn't made the move to get the hairdo, lose the weight, put in the work that led to the compliment, or made the decision in the first place?

It was you, after all, who took control of your destiny—if only for a minute. You took the risk; you reaped the reward.

If you'll admit that you had the power over that single minute, it must also hold that you have the power over a whole hour.

[See, every hour of our lives is just sixty of those single minutes.]

The way I figure it, my Sister, if you can multiply, you can be happy.

How simple can you get, Girlfriend?

When you stop taking your losses with Brothers so personally, you'll discover that love is its own reward.

You can count yourself among the lucky if you still have the capacity to fall in love. Some people have been so mauled in relationships that they no longer have the capacity to give love.

"Put that love out there often enough," said one Sister who married her Mr. Wonderful last year, "and it will boomerang back to you."

This Sister freely admitted that she'd been dumped too many times to count without a calculator. [No matter.] Although her campaign to corral a soulmate was a standing joke to her friends, Sister-Girl became adept at dusting herself off and hopping back in the ring like an American Gladiator before the whistle.

A secure and confident Sister is not afraid to love; she just knows when to stop. She doesn't have spare time for pining or whining about what she doesn't have or whom she is not with.

When you are involved in life, you are too busy getting out there to be shackled by insecurity.

You don't have time to feel sorry for yourself.

Since tomorrow is not promised, living each day to its fullest is guaranteed to chip away at the beast of insecurity until it is finally a slain dragon that lives only in your memory.

Since I've been a paragon of insecurity for most of my life, I feel super-qualified to tell my Sisters that you can get over it.

Here are the twenty affirmations that helped me slay my dragon.

TWENTY PERSONAL KEYS TO SLAYING THE BEAST OF INSECURITY

1. No one wants to hear a failure story. Build your own success story—from the inside out.
2. There are lessons to be learned in everything. Don't let your circumstances rob you of your joy.
3. God made all things different—for all time. Each of us has special and unique gifts. This means *you*—gift wrapped!
4. The past does not govern the future. You can change your course simply by changing your mind.

5. Daydreaming is an expensive waste of time. Remember, every fantasy has its price. You've got to pay to get into Disneyland.
6. Suffering is not permanent, and pain is not personal.
7. Jealousy is like a withered branch. It is ugly, useless, and only works to defeat the rest of a healthy tree.
8. Become a *tryaholic,* not a *failureholic.*
9. Every rejection brings you closer to an acceptance.
10. Grass will only grow in fertile soil.
11. An open mind leads to an open heart.
12. Losing your things may very well lighten your load.
13. Don't wait to save your best 'til next.
14. The opposite of good sense is nonsense.
15. The best thing is not what you are doing but what you are capable of doing.
16. She who hates cannot love.
17. Many opportunities come to us disguised as obstacles.
18. Right words create right impressions.
19. You can see the parade on television. But you can't smell the flowers without being there. Get involved.
20. Angels come! Believe, and create a soft place in your life where they can land.

4 THE 4-1-1 ON ATTRACTING ATTENTION: A HOW-TO AND WHERE-TO PRIMER

The signs are everywhere. Flirting is *in* in the nineties.

Have you noticed how some women flirt? It's not just with their eyes or their smile. The best flirtation is like swinging a tennis racquet, throwing a bowling ball, or executing a golf stroke. A woman who has mastered the sport of flirting throws her whole body into it.

A wink. A nod. A casual look—eyes big and bright, focused.

[Girlfriend has her follow-through *down.*]

Tossing her head gently, she laughs, showing off all those gleaming teeth that are her own. Her hair is fresh and clean and bobs when she gets excited.

[And you wonder why *Boyfriend* gets excited.]

She swings—like trees in the tropics—to the rhythm of her own nature. She is cool. She is refreshing. She is natural.

Nothing tense. No frozen tundra here.

Mind you, she is not in a do-or-die contest to get male attention. She's not competing—with anyone. The girl is just having fun and going with the flow.

You get the feeling that she's enjoying herself more than she is enjoying the attention she is generating.

Done right—with ease—flirting is an art form. And it is, oh, so much fun.

Men love women who can flirt. They can't get enough of it.

It's like a tasty appetizer, a little mouth moistener before the feast.

Sometimes I observe a group of women in a social or a business setting. [It's all the same, for the dating game and mating game are played wherever men and women meet.]

Wherever the games are played, one woman—in spite of her equally (or more) attractive, intelligent, and affluent Sisters—has the attention of all the men. She is obviously holding court in the house. And she is loving it.

This Sister doesn't care if you love her or loathe her. It is life that she embraces.

[But don't we react?]

Instead of riding this Sister, Girlfriend, let's learn something from her.

One day my salon was lit up on the subject of women with extreme sex appeal. Tastes ranged from Jane Fonda to Sheryl Lee Ralph. From Florence Griffith-Joyner to Whitney Houston. From Angela Lansbury to Lena Horne. From Halle Berry to Madonna.

[Now I understand why there are so many varieties of cereal on the supermarket shelf.]

Suddenly a confident young actress brought the gentlemen in their high-backed shine chairs to silence when she announced, "Any woman can be as sexy as Madonna. All she needs is the balls.

"Admit it," she cajoled, "the woman with balls is the one you want to put in your pocket."

[The gentlemen were aghast. She laughed. I got the feeling that she was knocking down strikes in her game of bowling for Brothers.]

"Believe you're the finest thing walking," she said, "and you *are* the finest thing walking. What is that but balls?"

The Sister wasn't really asking a question. She was making a point.

That's not profound, I said to myself. But what was profound was the attention the Sister was attracting. The Brothers sat there rapt, hanging on her every word, leaning forward with her every pause.

I think the Sister walked away with two or three phone numbers that day.

I know another cutie-pie Sister who can hold down a party of gentlemen by herself. Even when no other Sister is getting asked to dance, this confident Girlfriend has the Brothers lined up to the door.

"What's your secret?" I asked bluntly. "You're a good dancer, but please . . . "

She answered bluntly, "Any woman can be a good dancer. I'm a good *follower.*"

[Now, what is that but great balls of confidence?!]

I am convinced that men smell confidence, like a vulture smells blood or a dog smells meat. No matter what he says, man is carnivorous. It's in the species.

Let's pause on that confidence thing for a minute. Self-confidence, that is.

Self-confidence is not needing constant reassurance on your being OK. You neither need nor require the approval of another, no matter how significant that *other* is.

A friend of mine, as a young woman, was a natural athlete. A track star. Yes, *star!* She was one of the most gifted sprinters in her state, a hands-down contender for the Olympics. She devoted her life to track and field—developing healthy habits and the discipline to perform with excellence.

Most of us girls in PE class called her a tomboy, but the boys certainly got a kick out of her energy and spunk. Her muscular body was a *firecracker,* the guys joked.

She had at least five big brothers—the most gorgeous hunks on the track team, to the envy of the rest of us girls on the bench.

Until she stumbled into the vise of love, my friend was a sure bet. A winner. She was admired for her self-confidence and independence.

Her new boyfriend, however, insisted that his lady act more like a lady.

[Every word he uttered fanned the flames of her femininity.]

"Wear flattering shoes sometimes. Your legs look deformed in those old grandma shoes," he said.

That was only his first suggestion.

". . . And do something with your hair!"

"Listen," he said, after several months of heavy dating, "that track thing is taking up too much of your time."

[I wondered if Homeboy could have been jealous of my girl's five big brothers?]

"Why don't you give sports a rest and give us some time? You're so *good,* baby, that one semester won't matter . . . "

Well, the shot and the put of this story is that my friend did give up track to please her man.

Faster than you can say "final lap," she got pregnant. With the baby came the realization that her track career was over, and in her eyes, the Brother was to blame.

Quite soon after, the relationship was dissolved.

Girlfriend today is the hardworking single mother of two kids; she's tired and struggling, all of the freshness beat out of her like a high school practice track.

Her trophy room tarnished by bitterness, my friend, while still attractive, is no longer interesting to male suitors. She no longer exudes the graceful self-confidence of a winner.

Everybody loves a winner.

Winners are interesting. We all enjoy their stories of climbing out on a limb and their triumph over adversity.

When you lose your winning edge, you often lose your competitive edge as well.

While we're on the subject of winners, let me tell you about a gal who is now a successful dress designer.

This terrific single mom never felt sorry for herself, even when she was left with four small children by her husband of fifteen years.

She had only a high school education and no job.

What she *did* have was self-confidence.

[She wasn't afraid to bust a move.]

So she moved into a modest apartment, took a menial job, and cut back wherever she could in order to make ends meet.

She began her designing career as a means to clothe her kids inexpensively. With scraps of material, she would make something wild and imaginative. Then, with the scraps of scraps, she'd create something original for herself.

Together, this poor little family looked like a box of broken crayons.

Some people, I'm sure, laughed. But Girlfriend got so good at her patchwork designs that she was asked to make some originals for a few friends.

She was developing a following.

From a small group of patrons, she was able to buy better fabrics and modern equipment, attracting more and higher-paying customers.

. . . Customers, admirers, and eventually suitors. From suitors to a steady love. From a steady love to marriage.

I asked her husband of three years what had first attracted her to him, and he said, without pausing, "Her self-confidence makes her more alive than any woman I've ever met. That's what makes her so interesting."

To attract positive male attention a woman must be alive. And she must be interesting.

Interesting doesn't mean you have to memorize the latest Dow Jones averages or have a Ph.D. in geophysics from Princeton.

Interesting just means being interested and involved in life beyond self.

An *interesting* Sister has an active life with many experiences to share. She does not dwell on her personal tragedies. She takes the lumps and the sugar with aplomb.

Speaking of lumps, my Sister, we are not camels with our lumps out there for inspection. We've all got some bruises.

When you are hurting, you don't need the world to hurt with you on national television. A Brother who likes to dance through life will certainly not accept an invitation to your pity party.

Learn to have a sense of humor about yourself, whatever your circumstances. You and your circumstances can change.

Now that you've got the *how* of attracting positive male attention, let's talk about the *where*.

Where you go to meet a decent Brother these days is almost as important as being open to accept a positive relationship in the first place.

Obviously you won't attract the same kind of attention in a bar as you will in a bowling alley.

[Why are you surprised to find out that he's a practicing alcoholic when he told you that he works out at the club? Nightclub, that is.]

Now, about that bowling alley . . . Listen, Girlfriend, a bowling alley is a great place to meet a big-league player. Bowling alleys are the great melting pot of the male workforce. Practically every tenured bus driver, postal worker, and longshoreman I know belongs to a bowling league.

Speaking of bowling alleys, the least likely place to meet a decent catch is often the best place.

Not that you can't meet a great guy in a bar, but the chances are pretty slim. Men have come there, like you did, for the catch action. On the bar scene you'll usually find women are vying for male attention like groupies at a rock concert.

You can do better in places rarely frequented by women trying to get over. Like the bowling alley. Or the pool hall.

Or how about the barbershop?

You don't need a haircut and you don't have a son, you say?

Well, rent a son for a Saturday morning. Take your nephew

or your friend's son for a haircut and, afterward, breakfast at McDonald's.

You'll be doing a tired mom a service and maybe snip a little bonus for yourself.

Barbershops and shoe shine parlors—on Thursday, Friday, or Saturday—are great places to meet progressive men who are about something.

Now, I have mentioned shoe shine shops aplenty, but let me give you the 4–1–1 on this mecca of maledom.

Brothers who keep their shoes shined either have a job or are looking pretty darned hard for one. They are ambitious. They have an agenda. If they are not yet successful, you can bet that they are on the way.

Find the popular shoe shine parlor in your town and you'll also find the epicenter of the Brotherhood. Make yourself a regular. Don't be afraid to hop up into the arms of that comfortable high-backed leather chair for a shine.

For a couple of bucks you'll feel relaxed and look great from head to toe. And just think of the positive attention you'll be attracting.

Sure, some women may stare at you disapprovingly. But that's just because they don't have the nerve to take center stage.

To tell you the truth, Brothers are intrigued by Sisters who don't care what other women think. They know that the approval of our Sisterhood is the staple diet of our gender.

[Just think, all our gossip about a Sister is not doing anything but making her more intriguing to our men.]

While we're talking about gossip, my Sister, if you want to attract attention of the best kind, stay clear of poison words about anybody—your ex, your relatives, the woman across the street.

Any man worth his weight in cashmere knows that the cowardly lion roars the loudest.

He'll figure, and rightfully so, that a woman who talks about other people while trying to butter him up will one day spread the word thin on him too.

The best way to attract positive attention is to be joyous to the world, starting with yourself.

A happy tree bears healthy fruit.

And bad grapes produce bitter wine.

Now, back to that shoe shine parlor . . . or barbershop . . . or bowling alley: in the process of meeting new people you are also establishing new relationships and expanding your network of contacts.

As you build new relationships, one or two of them may turn into genuine friendships. So if you don't meet a love interest, at least you've met someone of interest. And who knows whom he knows?

Maybe the Brother has a friend. Or a cousin. Maybe the Brother has a brother!

Want some more unlikely places to meet men?

Everyone's hip to church. That's what I call the Old Standard. But have you ever thought of funerals?

I'm not trying to sound morbid. I'm really not! It just seems to me that death, everybody's final chapter, is definitely a part of life. You can't avoid it. So why not embrace the thoughtful tradition of paying your respects to your departed acquaintance?

Along with grieving family members, funeral services also comprise other friends, business associates, and coworkers of the deceased who have come to bid farewell. That means they are still very much alive.

[I have been assured by many of my Sisters who use funerals as a social event that those pews are virtually crawling with live ones!]

Along with bowling alleys, barbershops, shine parlors, funeral services, and wakes, I'd have to rank computer, camera, and electronic retail stores, car washes, garage sales, Laundromats, supermarkets, libraries (science and business sections), car shows, and bookstores as my favorite places to meet interesting men.

It has also been suggested by my sporty girlfriends that high school, YMCA, pro basketball games, golf courses, riding stables, and rifle ranges offer great action on and off the field.

All of these spots offer one thing: they are places where you can chat and get to know each other a tad without a swarm of women trying to make your private conversation a party line.

Party line. That reminds me of a theory proffered by a friend of mine, a vivacious lady who had returned to school at age forty-one for her law degree. She calls it the Catch a Fish theory.

She says, quite simply, "You can't catch a fish in a bathtub. You have to get out there in the deep water, where you can't touch bottom. The scarcest fish is in the deepest water, but it also brings the biggest prize."

Please believe me, on any given four-hour "fishing" expedition in a bar with your girlfriends, only one of you is likely to catch a live one.

So challenge me!

Reduce your odds of coming up with an old spare tire by fishing alone or at least in discreet company.

Your goal is, my Sister, to attract positive attention. Start by being positive. Don't just go anywhere. Go somewhere. And go with gusto and great relish.

Enthusiasm for who you are—what you're about and what you're into—are the qualities that make you an attractive attention-getter.

If you really want to attract male attention, you can drive a Beemer or a VW minibus, you can shop at designer salons or thrift shops, because the fact is you don't need to do or say anything extraordinary to impress him.

Just loosen up and relax and enjoy a Brother's attention, regardless of where you think it may lead.

Be feminine, attentive, and alive. And you will attract more quality male attention than you ever imagined possible.

5   "NICE"

There is a lot of ambivalence about nice guys. There is, in fact, ambivalence about *nice* anything.

Far from being a virtue, *nice* is often used in today's vernacular in place of "odd."

"That's a *nice* dress you're wearing" doesn't mean that your dress is pretty, sexy, or fashionable. "Nice" usually means that it looks like your dress is a third-generation hand-me-down. Or you bought it at a Salvation Army fire sale.

A *nice* car is cheap. A *nice* house is one no one else would want to live in.

When a friend suggests you meet her *nice* friend, you already know that he is boring and predictable.

A *nice* guy is the guy you love to hate. He is the nerd who hangs on you and around you until you kick him out of your life.

Nice guys finish last. If they finish at all.

When you are in a stormy relationship with one man, it is the other guy, the nice one, who is always your "incidental target." That is, you were aiming at someone else but the nice guy accidentally got in your line of fire. So he took the bullet. You didn't mean to hurt his feelings, to stand him up, to forget his birthday—it's just that something better came up. Or you forgot.

If you've got some ambivalent feelings about nice guys, you are in good company.

The ambivalence you feel probably stems from the confusion promulgated by the lexicographers themselves. Lexicographers, you see, spend their entire careers researching words, their meanings, and derivatives.

The great Noah Webster defines *nice* as "difficult to please; fastidious; refined."

Only at a spot way down the line—definition number six— does he say that *nice* is "agreeable; pleasant; and delightful."

Now, that's what Webster says.

The word comes from the Latin *nescius,* which means ignorant, not knowing.

Other dictionaries, like the *Oxford American,* define *nice* as "pleasant, satisfactory."

My thesaurus says that *nice* is "agreeable; amicable; congenial and friendly."

Is that confusing, or what?

I mean, if the people writing the dictionaries these days can't make up their minds on the meaning of *nice,* how the heck can we?

Maybe our root confusion over nice guys stems from our confusion over the root of the word *nice.*

You say he's so nice, but maybe you mean that he's so ignorant. Remember *nescius*?

That nice guy presents quite a dilemma for my Sisters.

Every normal, breathing single Sister *says* she is looking for a nice guy. Yet when she finds him, she treats him like the best friend of a new bride who tags along on the honeymoon.

Sure, he's a man with feelings, and she doesn't really want to lose him. But then, on the other hand, she wonders why he hangs around where he's not wanted.

Another problem with nice guys: because they're there, it's tempting to do unto them as you've been done unto.

If you're being jerked around by some heel, sometimes you just have to give someone else the boot!

A nice guy tells you that he is willing to wait forever for you to return his affections. You want to scream, "That's exactly how long it will take."

The jerks, women, and the nice guys themselves all agree on one thing: nice guys get no respect.

Nice today means a Brother is gullible, stupid, and conspicuously accessible.

[No wonder nice guys finish last.]

Maybe it's time to get this "nice" thing straight.

A nice guy is one who takes you dancing. A nice guy will go with you to walk the dog. He doesn't mind seeing your hair in rollers. He brings his money home. He listens.

A nice guy shows up, can be counted on, and genuinely cares what you think.

One contented Sister told me that her nice guy is considerate—of her time, her feelings, and her goals.

Another, a high-strung musician, claims that what makes her nice guy so special is his tolerance of her many moods.

Not one of these Sisters would look at another man. They love being treated grandly.

I have several friends who married nice guys. To tell the truth—to a woman—they've never been happier.

How they met their Mr. Nice Guy varied, but all of these Sisters agreed that they picked up some other woman's leavings.

[Leftovers.]

He was banged around by another Sister so badly that he hid from women by spending all his free time working on his car or buffing up at the gym.

In the nineties, nice guys are so discouraged they have all but taken themselves out of the race to attract nice ladies. They've grown so quiet we hardly know they still exist.

[Darned that old Webster! He's got our relationships all screwed up.]

Nice guys make the best catches. There is no contest. Not only is a nice guy a pleasant enough fellow to be around, he is available.

And there's the big bonus. A nice Brother stopped looking for perfection long ago. You don't have to constantly dazzle him or use all your energy to confound him. This cordial gent just wants a lady who will treat him with a little respect.

There are a lot of nice guys out there, my Sister, if only you'll change your *himpressions* about what *nice* means to you.

If you have a nice Brother scoping you out, you had better put on your glasses. Please learn to pamper him before some other sharp-eyed Sister with twenty-twenty sets her sights on him.

6 IF YOU CAN BUILD A GENERATOR, I'LL FOLLOW YOU (ALMOST) ANYWHERE

'll be the first one to admit that I can't do anything without simple grade school instructions. I can't program a digital clock, set a VCR, or defrost in a microwave oven with any more complicated directions than "Start" and "Stop." [Preferably with metallic numbered arrows to guide me.]

I am a prisoner in my home when it comes to the simplest of tasks or repairs—changing a vacuum cleaner bag, installing a towel rack, or getting that dang garbage disposal to work.

In today's modern office everything is perplexing to me, except the light switch and the elevator button.

[Please don't ask me about hardware, software, modems, or mouses.]

My automobile, needless to say, is as enigmatic as nuclear fission.

[I've even met some car stereos I couldn't turn on.]

There's just no escaping it: I am ignorant in all things mechanical, electronic, or technical. I am a macro-micro-electro-cellular-digital dummy.

Even today's instructions are a jumble to my simple mind. Although packaged directions look like they're written in English—all the letters are there—I can understand no more than a dozen words, like "WARNING" and "If you need additional assistance, call our 800 number."

In all these years, I've learned only one thing when I get in over my head with handiwork—and that's how to turn something O-F-F.

I figure I'm such an admitted klutz in any task that involves manual-mechanical-technical-electronic labor because my education followed the traditional sexist sixties party line. Home economics, typing, and choir were the recommended electives for girls.

[Who'd be caught dead in a shop class?]

Today I envy anyone who can change a tire, rewire anything, or repair a household appliance.

I stand in awe of a person who can assemble a kid's bike, install a ceiling fan, or build a kitchen cabinet.

In the forty-odd years that I've recognized that there is a difference between men and women, I've never appreciated the prowess of the opposite sex as much as I do now, in this complicated age of intelligent technology—in which I feel pretty stupid.

[As I crawl up the on-ramp of the information superhighway, I am certain that I'll need a lifetime membership for roadside service.]

Now, Girlfriend, if you've ever been stranded or stalled in traffic without a clue as to what's wrong with your vehicle, doesn't it give you a rush to see the beautiful flashing lights of a AAA tow truck comin' your way? At that moment, Mike the Mechanic looks quite a bit like Wesley Snipes.

[For Mike the Mechanic, a sincere smile from a stylishly suited Sister is better than a six-pack in summer. And don't let Girlfriend be driving a Lexus or a Saab! We're talkin' imported brew for the boys in blue!]

Since embarking on this great crusade to pamper the Blackman, I've come to believe that the best men to pamper are the men who work darned hard for the little pampering they do get, the guys we barely notice or shoo away with a wave of our cell phones, the gentle gents who keep our cars running, our offices humming, and our homes from falling apart.

I say, three cheers for the blue-collar working stiffs—the carpenters, linesmen, installers, grease monkeys, and computer jockeys who keep our lives in tune and on track.

Let's roll out the red carpet for the full- and part-time home-project warriors and fix-it freaks who have an absolute grip on saving money by doing it themselves.

To me there is nothing sexier than a man who can do it himself. I get off on the rough callused hands of a working man. [And a pair of tight, worn Levis, torn in all the right places. Have mercy!]

I'll take grease under the fingernails over a manicured hand anytime.

[Who wants a man with hands softer than yours, anyway?]

For a survivalist like me, in earthquake-prone California, having an independent power supply in case of catastrophe is more practical than having a decent bank account.

[A flood will sho' nuff wipe out your funds.]

My philosophy about this matter of men is this: if you can build a generator, I'll follow you almost anywhere.

When I'm in the eye of a hurricane, I don't want to be with anyone who is weaker than me and is going to panic.

[Be my hero. OK? My hat is off to anyone who is a master of anything nonacademic.]

So for you guys who can install plumbing or rehinge a door, add a room, repair a car, tile a floor, or build a fence—it's time to stick your chests out. This chapter is for you!

Now, one corporate lawyer lady whom I admire told me that she'd been romanced on land, in the air, and by sea—in restaurants, on private yachts, and in airplanes—by white-collar Homeboys spending buckets full of money trying to impress her.

It was all ho-hum until she met a blue-collar Brother who

enjoyed handiwork. The romantic evening she remembers most was a moonlight barbecue under the stars with the man who had just enclosed and painted her patio and wired a sound system throughout her house.

Girlfriend said that she appreciated her new beau even more a few months later when she learned that the equity in her home had been boosted by the improvements.

Another young recent MBA grad (who has a ton of student loans to repay) puts it this way: "A ride in a man's new Porsche tonight doesn't help my old Toyota get cranked up tomorrow morning."

[For more and more professional women in the nineties, a man who can change a tire, put in an oil filter, and tune up a car is worth his weight in beauty supply products.]

I'm meeting many interesting professional women these days who have met their soulmates in nurseries, auto-parts and hardware stores, lumber and equipment rental yards.

[Now that's home improvement!]

I've got nothing against those three-piece-suit dudes. Really! It's just that in my book, manicures and masonry just don't mix.

I'm sorry, but too many Brooks Brothers Brothers I know think that their earnings keep women yearning. I try to tell Sisters that in today's tightfisted global economy, we'd do better to get our thrills from a man with manual skills.

I've been wondering why the wool-and-tweed boys get all the attention while our blue-collar buddies barely get honorable mention with most Sisters these days.

Ladies—especially educated types who've spent all their time in books and board rooms—need to look at the pool of eligible Brothers who can use their hands for more than just pulling out a credit card.

I say it's time, after years of neglect, for Sisters to applaud our hardworking hard-hatters. I say hip-hip-hooray for any man who can climb a pole or dig a hole.

These Brothers in starched uniforms are on the march as they deliver our mail and our bottled water. They travel the highways and byways carrying precious cargo to our homes, offices, farms, and stores.

They stoke the fires of America's remaining factories, and then they put those fires out in our ravaged forests. They tear down the old, level the land, and build up the new.

They can dig a ditch and pitch a tent. They can pound a nail and lift a pail. And that's just on their first shift!

Personally, I think America stopped working when the good ol' boys in the executive suites handed the boys in the yard their pink slips.

[All of our engines groaned to a halt.]

Since the dawning of the Information Age, our blue-collar Brothers have gradually learned to hide their manual skills from the rest of the world.

[Where'd those skills get them during the company's reconfiguration?]

Many a macho man has covered his tattoos with a starched shirt and sports jacket. He's learned to tolerate fluorescent lights and office air-conditioning. Even when it comes to doing the things he loves, he's learned to keep quiet and call maintenance.

Since Sisters started putting them down in the sixties (when it was no longer cool to date a man who wore work boots and got his hands dirty), these Brothers became chameleons—darting behind Friday-night football and a series of excuses for why they couldn't install the venetian blinds. The truth is, they were bored. Bored and unappreciated.

Today, in the thick of the Information Age, the only information most Sisters want is, where are our blue-collar Brothers?

The answer, sadly, is as close as our computer screens.

In abandoning our blue-collar Brothers—their crude ways and hard hands—Sisters have driven them totally underground.

In the sixties and seventies, we put them down for their baseball caps, Red Wing work boots, and pickup trucks. We criticized their simple crafts and protested their complex projects. We laughed at their labor and scoffed at their skills.

We could not pardon them for the sin of tracking mud through the house. Or of making holes in their white cotton socks. And we hated them for leaving grease on our embossed towels.

["What'd you think I am, the maid?"]

We sweated the seasons of insecurity when work at the plant or in the yard was slow. And we spent all the money when the work wasn't slow.

In trying to eradicate a few weeds in our relationships, Sisters used Agent Orange on the egos of our blue-collar Brothers.

[We killed everything in the yard *except* the weeds.]

By rejecting our grimy guys, we've turned our attention toward sanitized, dust-free dudes who thought that manual labor was uncorking the wine. In word and deed, we have strip-mined the field of blue-collar boys and laid them to waste.

Now, what happens when a predator has no competition?

In the eighties our blue-collar Brothers either joined the enemy or gave up the fight to the white-collar boys.

The predatory white collars, of course, took full advantage of the retreat and the absence of the blues. That was their chance to overwhelm all adversaries.

[They learned that strategy in business school, don't you know.]

What we have now—in the nineties, at the gateway to the twenty-first century—is a bear in a goldfish bowl. Those white-collar boys are really throwing their weight around. So now they think they've won this war.

[Our situation, ladies, is sorta like the classic Western, *High Noon,* with Gary Cooper. The enemy is overwhelming.]

But I just want to say—here and now, once and for all—that although the clock is still ticking, we've still got five minutes to high noon.

Of course, my vision of *High Noon* has changed a bit to keep up with the times. Instead of Gary Cooper bringing the bad guys to justice, I see the "3-Ds" rising superbly to the occasion. The "3-Ds"—that's Danny Glover, Denzel Washington, and Dr. Dre.

In my fantasy, Danny, Denzel, and Dre parachute into a town of womenfolk left defenseless and overwhelmed by the ruthless and greedy White-Collar Gang.

The "3-Ds" blow their work whistles and suddenly a brigade of Blue-Collar Brothers throw down their ballpoint pens, tear off their sports jackets, and stampede through the double glass doors of the law firm.

They charge, spilling into the streets, with a welder's whoop and a longshoreman's yelp—letting nothing stand in their way. Not the downturned economy that claimed their high-paying hourly jobs, nor the marauding White-Collar Gang, whose members limit their lines of credit and steal their women after the foreclosure.

Look yonder, Sisters, beyond the high-tech horizon: see the "3-Ds" leading their strapping kinsmen in building new and improved services, retrofitting industries and trades that are going begging for some ambitious Blue-Collar Brother to ply.

In my vision, the Blue-Collar Brothers, armed with shovels, picks, tool boxes, and miles of electrical tape, are coming out of the closet (the one that they, in fact, constructed) to restake a claim on their American dream and, in the process, to rescue thousands of Sisters in great distress.

In the spirit of healthy competition, I challenge my brawny Blue-Collar Brothers to take up their anvils, their chain saws, their T-squares, and their generators.

Go home, my Brothers. Come back home, my buddies in blue jeans. Build a home, my husky heroes.

On behalf of an untold number of Sisters who are just too proud to beg, I beseech you, dear downsized dudes: tune up our engines, weatherproof our windows, and restucco our crumbling walls.

Stop singin' the blues, and start livin' in them, dear Blue-Collar Brothers. Be proud of who you are. Reclaim your position in our human family, and assume your place at the head of our preassembled tables.

Whisk us affluent, triple-degreed, Maxima-driving, Armanisuit-wearing, lonely Sisters away from the ballet to a hoedown that is low-down.

Serenade us with your staple guns, your plumber's snakes, your wire, and your Allen wrenches. Give us a bouquet made of tool bits, wrapped in blueprints.

Hammer your way home, my blue-collar heroes. We'll throw away the Drano if you'll please unclog our drains.

Come on home, dear sweaty sweethearts. No one can take your place.

7 ONE HUNDRED AND ONE WAYS TO PAMPER YOUR BLACKMAN

Now, don't get overwhelmed. One hundred and one of anything can be overwhelming. But you got this far, Sister-Girl. [You are already way past fail-safe. You might as well read on.]

Now you don't have to complete all 101 suggestions of this Pampering Manifesto in order to satisfy your Blackman's appetite for sweets. But please remember, ladies, *his* appetites are what we're talking about here, and all 101 suggestions have been tested by Sisters as they pursued their mastery of the confectionery arts.

Nothing on this pamper list is frightfully expensive or even time-prohibitive. In fact, the best of these suggestions are free and take just minutes for you to perform.

These are not like mental gymnastics—you don't even have to sweat. Just use your imagination, and in no time you'll have him eating out of your hands!

1. Ask. Don't beg or demand.
2. Compliment him on his accomplishments.
3. Be confident and self-sufficient.
4. Prepare a candlelight dinner with all his favorite things.
5. Draw a scented candlelight bath for him (or for both of you).
6. Buy him flowers or a nice plant for his office.
7. Give him peace.
8. Organize his closet or sock drawer.
9. Keep yourself clean.
10. Surprise him with a manicure and pedicure.
11. Take his mother to lunch.
12. Buy him cologne or aftershave.
13. Laugh with him, never at him.
14. Keep your bag of sexual tricks and treats full.
15. Be considerate of his idiosyncrasies.
16. Don't try to change him radically.
17. Send him a fantasy fax or leave a sexy message on his voice mail.
18. Take him to a movie.
19. Cheer him on at his basketball games or in his bowling league.
20. Listen to him.
21. Tell him a story or read aloud to him.
22. Give him a massage.
23. Give him a foot massage.
24. Write love notes and hide them in his personal things.
25. Want the best for him.
26. Use your skills to help him plan his career and make his career moves.
27. Watch TV with him.
28. Don't gossip.
29. Have his favorite photo blown up and framed.
30. Clean his smudgy glasses with glass cleaner.
31. Buy him a new toothbrush when you notice the old one fraying.
32. Ask him to teach you something, and take a real interest in learning it.

33. Encourage him.
34. Be sexy.
35. Be spontaneous and exciting.
36. Notice what's new about him.
37. Do a striptease.
38. Learn to be a good cook.
39. Have meals ready on time.
40. Keep a clean, well-stocked kitchen.
41. Wear perfume—on your body and in your hair.
42. Tell him a modern-day fairy tale in which he is the hero of the story.
43. Don't sulk.
44. Take him on a date.
45. Dance with him.
46. Don't remind him of his failures.
47. Love him for who he is.
48. Surprise him with his name on a removable tattoo in a secret place on your body.
49. Limit your time on the phone.
50. Apply a warm iron to his towel while he showers and sprinkle it with cologne. Have it waiting for him when he steps out of the shower.
51. Be polite.
52. Look at him when he's speaking.
53. Fix his coffee or tea and offer to bring it to him.
54. Cherish your time together.
55. Encourage him to stay within his budget, and don't be the cause of his overspending.
56. Cut out articles from the newspaper he'll be interested in.
57. Call his mother to say hello.
58. Write him a thank-you note.
59. Take him on a picnic.
60. Put the cap on the toothpaste.
61. Don't put his business in the streets.
62. Respect his privacy.
63. Allow him to have friends.

64. Don't snoop.
65. Buy him an X-rated magazine for the two of you to share.
66. Be faithful.
67. Respect him in front of your friends.
68. Give him a kiss for no reason.
69. Treat his ex-wife, the mother of his children, with respect.
70. Spend time with his kids.
71. Need and heed his advice.
72. Say what you mean and mean what you say.
73. Never share your secrets with anyone else.
74. Buy him a present for no reason.
75. Prepare a gourmet lunch for him to take to work.
76. Catalog his videocassettes.
77. Don't leave your hair in the bathroom washbasin.
78. Create a dessert and name it after him.
79. Check his shoes for shines and laces.
80. Take his clothes to the cleaners.
81. Never compare him to anyone.
82. Lip-synch his favorite love song, with all the drama you can invent.
83. When you apologize, mean it.
84. Serve him breakfast in bed.
85. Keep a record of his special family commemorations—birthdays, graduations, anniversaries, and deaths.
86. Stockpile a few greeting cards for him to use for his family remembrances.
87. Be his friend.
88. Don't nag or complain.
89. Encourage him to stay fit and healthy.
90. Learn how to tie his tie for him.
91. Encourage him to dream.
92. Even after you've won his heart, flirt with him.
93. Plant a tree in his honor.
94. Praise him to his children.
95. Make him "King for a Day."
96. Be mindful of his moods.

97. Save a few dollars each week for a surprise weekend get-away.
98. Be forgiving and don't hold grudges.
99. Make him a Christmas or Valentine's Day card.
100. Clean his comb and brush.
101. Pray for him and with him.

8 PICKING AND CHOOSING, OR ONE WOMAN'S HASH IS ANOTHER'S GOURMET FEAST

You can't make a pot of chili without having the ingredients. And you won't have all the ingredients until you go to the store.

Ladies, the market shelves are well stocked. Please don't settle for the first hunk of hamburger you set your sights on.

Now, this is a tough one for some Sisters—even in the midst of today's AIDS terror.

My mother used to tell me, and most mothers still tell their sexually curious daughters, "Keep your panties on."

"But I love him," you say.

[Believe me, if you walk into like before you fall into love, you will make wiser choices. Remember that love is blind. So how are you going to shop with your eyes closed?]

A Catholic nun (of all callings) once shared with me the secret of a successful marriage: "Select a partner with the qualities you most desire in a mate," she said. "Throw out the L-word entirely. If he makes you happy—satisfying your personal needs—believe me, you'll fall in love with him."

I followed this divine logic in considering my second husband, accepting his proposal even though I didn't love him in that boom-boom way that makes your blood rush.

He was a nice man and a great friend who made me laugh. We had wonderful, adventurous fun, and we had much in common. I didn't love him, but I really *liked* him.

Within a month of being married—as we planned our belated honeymoon to Rio de Janeiro for Carnival—I fell in love with this kind and thoughtful man. That love only grew in time and never wavered.

We had a successful marriage for ten years, until other obstacles loomed.

Now, before your *like* oozes into *love,* and you know that you have his attention, let's examine why you're seeking his attention in the first place.

Is he really the one you want, or are you just window-shopping at the after-Christmas sale?

Now you know, Girlfriend, that we have a bad habit of buying a pair of shoes just because they're cute and in style, our girlfriend likes them, or they're on sale.

If they hurt, we may wear them only once. Or we'll wait to buy a perfect dress to match. Usually, though, those expensive brand-new shoes will sit in the back of the closet until we give them away.

Let's be honest. Sometimes a Sister will treat a man like those cute pair of new shoes that she really didn't want in the first place.

[If you do anything more than try him on, you've let your vanity overrule your sanity.]

You think you may like him (someday). But you know you're wrong to be using the poor fellow to catch Mr. Right.

[Am I wrong?]

What goes around comes around.

★　　　★　　　★

So now you finally meet someone interesting. You like the Brother, and you think he has the same feelings for you.

You think you are his girlfriend, but you may only be an amusing diversion from his problems at work, problems at home, or problems with people.

To this rakish rogue, you are just a pair of "cute shoes."

One attractive and wealthy gentleman whom I adored used to take me to expensive restaurants four or five times a week.

I thought he genuinely loved me.

The truth was that he genuinely loved to eat, and I was good company—like a fine linen napkin on his lap.

Some men hate to eat alone!

Some men hate to do anything alone. You are only in their lives to fill up the empty spaces.

One of my greatest loves was such a man. After six months of blissful dating, he began to "pick" arguments out of me, like a cat owner picking fur balls out of the sofa.

Suddenly I could do nothing right. Nothing pleased him. He was truly unhappy.

I discovered that he really loved the shifting sands of chaos. For a short time I was, for him, a large smooth rock in the stream that he could use to keep his feet dry.

He finally married a lady who satisfied his insatiable hunger for pain. She was a sweet young Georgia peach of a girl whom he subsequently hospitalized after one of their frequent, nasty spats.

She, in turn, upon her release and return home, tried to fry him in hot chicken grease while he slept.

Wake up, ladies, and smell the roses. The garden is filled with infinite variety. You don't have to settle for artificial flowers.

You don't have to be miserable in a relationship.

"A man at any cost," my Sister, is a strategy out of the 1950s that our mothers used to earn that house with a white picket fence.

These are the nineties, and most of us live in apartments,

condos, and townhouses anyway. Isn't it time to choose to be in a satisfying relationship?

Some ladies only pick men who are inaccessible. Married men, gay men, convicts, priests, and just-divorced men are all clearly inaccessible. Yet some Sisters seem hell-bent on chasing these Brothers.

Like a piece of ripening fruit, you can usually tell a man who is pickable. He (a) is generally honest about his involvements, (b) is usually open to suggestions on how you spend your time together, and (c) always enjoys your company. He returns your affections in equal or greater measure.

I have a friend who has been in love with more married men than there are pigeons on a playground. She says that's not her intention. But when we sat down to talk about the dilemma that seemed to keep her mascara running, she broke down.

It was the mystique of chasing a man who didn't want her that was the turn-on and the challenge. Her "high" came from being near a man who was just out of reach.

Many women thrive on the chase. They don't want a man who has his feet planted on the ground. These Sisters seem deliberately to choose . . .

The Benz-o-Drivin' Lady-Killer, whose "little black book" looks like the Manhattan Yellow Pages

The Professional Man, whose every sentence starts with "I" or "my"

The Career Criminal or Chronically Unemployed

The long-suffering Tormented Alcoholic or Drug Addict

The Pathetic Puppy whose luck just won't change

The neat-to-the-bone, lint-free Eternal Bachelor

The Married-to-Mama Man

Or his cousin, the My-Kids-Can-Do-No-Wrong Parent-Man.

Don't think I'm talking Psychology 101 here, good Sisters. I've been in relationships with all of these untouchables. And I have the battle scars to prove it.

My nemesis seems to be the Pathetic Puppy type. They aren't overtly mean or insensitive. They are chameleon-type men who appear to be normal nice guys. But they are nice guys who, unfortunately, have been kicked so hard by life that they have permanent hoof marks on their egos.

One beau, whom I simply adored, had been an abused husband for seventeen years. Although divorced for six years, he recounted past historical atrocities as if they'd been in yesterday's newspaper.

Every now and then he'd go on a tirade. The memory of his unfaithful wife would suddenly cloud our pleasant present moments.

The more he relaxed with me, the more he'd experience psychedelic flashbacks to his tormented past relationship.

One night, in a casual dinner setting, as I was suggesting items on the menu, he shouted, "Shut up!"

I knew it wasn't me he was talking to but rather the ghost of his devious and deceitful ex-wife. But still, who can compete with a ghost? I'm not in the exorcism business.

Another fine, robust, and intelligent friend of mine was caught up in job stress. Once again he appeared to be normal. But on further inspection, there were tire marks across the face of his self-esteem that looked like the tire tracks of a bumper car ride at Tinkertown.

[Screech!]

The closer we got, the more comfortable he was taking me on his bumpy ride of rejection by Corporate America. Slipping in and out of his horror story, he put on the brakes only to tell me how he planned to get even.

I had to turn him off just to keep my own engine running.

If you pick a Pathetic Puppy, be sure, my Sister, you are ready to provide constant maternal vigilance.

These guys are never housebroken and will not hesitate to tinkle on your rug. They are never sorry, and they are always pitiful.

And when you abandon them, expect to be charged with inhumane treatment and animal endangerment.

Now before we leave the kennel, Girlfriend, and the downside of our choices, let's talk about the *Dogcatcher*.

That's what I call ladies whose only experiences are with heels, jerks, and ne'er-do-wells who will take a Sister for anything (and everything) they can get.

I hear the horror stories from all sides: the "dogs" who only pimp broads, the ladies who are being treated like bitches, and the nice guys who try to rescue them.

If he is a big spender, flashy dresser, or a charismatic fast-talker, those are just a few signs that your new show dog may still belong in the kennel.

Here's my famous "Dogcatcher Quiz" designed to identify a Sister who always attracts men who are heartbreakers.

ARE YOU A DOGCATCHER?

1. Are you into thrills (this does not necessarily mean adventure)?
2. Are you bored if he doesn't have a good line?
3. Does your first date or first kiss have to crinkle your toes and turn your brain to mush?
4. Would you rather have his money than his time?
5. Does his car, house, dog, or job overly impress you?
6. Are you into Power (with a capital P)?
7. Does his style hold more of your attention than his smile?
8. Does it bother you if he stutters, stammers, or is clumsy when he tells you how much he cares for you?
9. Does getting laid mean more to you than being loved?
10. Would you rather have his gold than share his goals?

If you answer "yes" to any one of these questions, I'd seriously look at yourself as a possible Dogcatcher. You're inviting trouble into your own backyard.

My advice is to have the Brother tested for rabies before you take him home to play with the kids.

★   ★   ★

I have found some truth to the homespun adage "You get what you deserve." You definitely attract what you want by affirming it in thought, word, and action.

And listen, Girlfriend, don't put a label or a name on your eventual soulmate. Be open and flexible. You think he's *the one* today, but Mr. Tom, Richard, or Hakim may not be your intended life's partner in the thousand tomorrows ahead of you.

Our picture of the present moment is limited. God's picture is of the universe for all the time that was, is, and ever will be. Now which picture do you trust?

There *is* someone for everyone. In fact, there is more than one someone for everyone. To prove it, look at your own life experiences. How many times have you loved someone so hard you thought you would break if they didn't love you back?

And when you didn't break and didn't die but lived to love again, weren't you a tad surprised?

[Come on, Girl, admit it.]

In my little corner of the world, I personally know hundreds of fine eligible men of all ages, races, and professions—many looking for meaningful relationships.

If this little corner is any kind of sample, I am sure that there is someone for everyone!

It is your life. It is your choice. Today, pick this moment to be happy. Choose this time to be accessible to the good that is waiting for you around the corner.

And while you negotiate the twists and turns along the highway of life, I wish you happy motoring, my Sister. May you enjoy safe driving conditions to your destination.

9 THE KITCHEN IS OPEN, BUT THERE'S NO FREE LUNCH

I don't care how much the Brother cares for you, Girlfriend, you can cancel yourself out of his life by pushing his credit to the limit. That Visa or American Express Gold card he's carrying is only plastic, not flesh and brawn.

The proof of a relationship is not the sum of its plastic parts. Shake him financially, and he's sure to break you emotionally.

Now, he knows that you know caviar from catfish and veal from Vienna sausage, but what are you trying to prove by ordering the most expensive meal on the menu without any consideration of his budget?

[Forget his rent, his child support, or car payment. Only the meal's for real in this deal.]

I have a friend who prides herself on how much it costs a gentleman to keep her entertained. She is on a first-name basis with every maitre d' from New York to New Orleans. And not because *she's* picking up the tab.

The speculation is that this selfish Sister is a culinary courtesan, a gastronomic Mata Hari who won't leave a Brother with anything in his pocket but a mint and a toothpick.

★　　★　　★

Another Sister—an attractive thirtysomething lady who couldn't tell you her Social Security number—takes pride in telling anyone who'll listen about her one hundred pairs of shoes, who bought them, and how much he paid.

[This Sister is not a clotheshorse—she is a clothes whore! Why, she barely wears the same outfit once.]

Her whole house, I'm told, is furnished in early African-American art—Tom, Dick, and Malik.

[The pad must look like a museum of past relationships.]

There are two types of Sisters who almost never get their man: the Greedy Sister and the Needy Sister. Let me tell you, Girl, the kitchen is still open, but they're not serving free lunch.

Wine and dine her, and the Greedy Sister will eat 'til she throws up. Her only focus is on how much she can get.

Now, when you take the Needy Sister to dinner, she'll finish her food, but she'll take home three more entrées in a doggy bag.

I'll grant you that it's easy to be hungry for a little pampering yourself in these uneasy and uncertain times.

[We are all scared to death, OK?]

I've got to admit that it's awfully easy to be greedy if you've gotten used to being needy.

[He may offer to make barbecue at your house, but isn't it tempting to ask him to buy a new grill?]

I'll certainly admit that the average Sister today is needy. She is a single parent, trying to make ends meet with no help from the kids' father.

[Can I get a witness?]

Say you've got two kids in school. One needs braces; the other is in Little League. You're working two jobs trying to make it. Still you've got to sit on that old furniture. And you drive an old car that breaks down every other week. You haven't bought a new dress for yourself in three years.

[Are you a great fake, or what?]

Wouldn't it be nice, for a change, to have a man give you something besides a hard time? Maybe buy you a little luxury or two? Treat you to a weekend in the woods? A shopping spree?

[OK, even a new pair of stockings that you don't have to pay for!]

I had a girlfriend who was dating a swell Brother who had a secure job, a little IRA, and a decent life insurance policy. He wasn't rich, mind you, but he lived comfortably with his sister and her teenage son.

My friend started seeing green after he spent one pleasant weekend in her well-appointed suburban Tudor-style home (it was her payoff in a costly divorce settlement).

She had the Brother fixing her leaky faucets, hanging pictures, buying groceries and fertilizer for her exotic houseplants.

The following weekend cost him a couple of CDs, a towel set, and three bottles of imported water—in addition to taking her out two nights running.

Within the month, by her own estimate, the good Brother had spent over a thousand dollars on her, not counting his labor.

Nevertheless, the only cooking this Sister did was in the bedroom. She reckoned that he was not a guest in her home, but rather she was providing him weekend room and board.

This ill-advised Sister saw herself as saving him, not costing him. Sister-Girl obviously forgot that he didn't have to be there.

[Brother Man already had a place to lay his head and get his mail.]

She was, in retelling how she had "gotten over," quite proud of the job she had worked on "her" man, without him even knowing it.

A few months later she sadly reported that she and the Brother were no longer an item. Today, she is, I'm afraid, back to mowing her own lawn.

★ ★ ★

Now, I'm not saying that every gesture of kindness a Brother makes has to be reciprocated. All I'm saying is that if you want to create a positive *himpression,* be considerate of his wallet, his time, and the energy he is dedicating to your relationship.

Better to order the house wine and enjoy the blush of your new romance than to demand a vintage French wine that will make his budget blush.

Speaking of dinner, this is an area where it's a good idea to show reciprocity, to take him out for dinner once in a while. Or if your budget won't allow, cook for him every few dates. Men love a good home-cooked meal—especially perennial bachelors who have several restaurant menus committed to memory.

[These guys are so microwave-friendly they even nuke the soup.]

If you ask a Brother what he misses most about his mother, he'll usually say, "Her cooking."

That should tell you something!

Now, a word about taking him out. It's not like you have to spend a fortune to prove that you care. You don't have to spring for tickets to an Anita Baker concert or a gourmet feast.

Every town has a fun joint, a little truck stop (frequently off the beaten track) that's loaded with color, atmosphere, *and* low prices.

[He *can't* pick anything on the menu that costs more than $5.95!]

Don't apologize for holding to your budget. Be just as proud of the $5.95 you spend on him as he is the $59.95 he spent on you the night before.

[Girlfriend, please understand that you don't have to match him to catch him.]

And while we're on the subject of pampering through the palate, don't forget that as the weather warms, it is a perfect time for picnics.

You can plop your basket down virtually anywhere: in the park, the woods, at the beach, or by the lake.

I once took a date on a picnic in a cemetery. Well, not just any cemetery. It was Forest Lawn Memorial Park—a bucolic setting in a sea of green lawn and trees, surrounded by squirrels, swans, and waterfalls.

After this out-of-this-world experience I couldn't beat the Brother off with a Ouija board.

The point is, you don't need to spend his last dime or yours to hold a Brother's interest.

Listen, Girlfriend, you have to know how to play it.

Now, if the Brother makes a suggestion, it's perfectly all right to accept a gift. But if a shopping list comes from your lips, it may be one of the last requests you utter before he disappears into the aisles and gets himself lost in line.

If shopping is your turn-on, pamper him into thinking that it's *his* idea. Offer to cook him dinner and have him help you to shop for the things *he* likes.

In this way, if you sneak in a few goodies for yourself (like vitamins, bath salts, or lotion), you won't look so greedy. Or needy. You won't *appear* to be desperate.

I totally blew that *appearance* thing one otherwise-romantic evening when a gentleman friend offered to buy me flowers. I asked him instead if he'd take me to the drug store for a bottle of Vitamin C.

[I didn't need flowers. I did need Vitamin C.]

He agreed but was dismayed. We stopped dating a short time after this embarrassing incident.

There's no telling how far you can throw a little subtlety.

Subtlety is what Brothers see in Southern girls. They know how to take an idea and make a man claim it as his own.

The same goes for Asian women and, yes, White women.

[There, I've said it.]

I've seen White women work their mojoes on our Brothers without so much as working up a sweat. For many of them, pampering the Blackman is as easy as putting on a pair of panty hose.

While many Sisters are throwing out evil looks and wild words to get what they want, ladies of other cultures are getting mileage out of a smile, a little encouragement, approval, recognition, a kiss hello or a kiss good-bye.

[OK, so how many roto-head hoochie mamas do you know who can hold on to a man past midnight?]

There's no telling how far a little kindness will go with our Brothers. If you have a problem giving more than is absolutely required in your relationship with a Brother, I urge you to watch how some women can get an open line of credit in the bank of love, while other women have to pay to play and pay interest besides.

[Now, who do you think is getting shortchanged?]

Pampering the Blackman today is like the Red Cross serving the victims of any modern-day tragedy. There is always a point at which giving a little more makes more than a little difference.

A Sister who has truly mastered the art of pampering her relationships knows that it is the giving that is the gift.

10 BEWARE THE FAAWABA!

It helps, when we're talking about pampering, to understand the antithesis of this fine noble art. To this end I say, Beware the FAAWABA!

WARNING: A FAAWABA is a woman who threatens to undermine the little opportunity other Sisters have to pamper a Brother by totally destroying the trust he has in *all* women.

I digress.

To conquer the enemy, you must know who she is.

If you think the FAAWABA is a species of fierce jungle beast with few predators and an insatiable appetite for living flesh, you'd be perfectly right.

F.A.A.W.A.B.A. That's an acronym for *Ferocious African-American Woman with a Bad Attitude*. These Sisters are by no means extinct and are in every way dangerous.

I'll start by pointing the finger back at myself. During periods of great upheaval and personal dissatisfaction, I've been a FAAWABA princess through many relationships.

Since I speak from some experience, I can tell you that a FAAWABA is not someone you want to mess with. She will give you headaches and strokes, make you lose your hair or your mind. She is Jezebel, without any mask of propriety.

For the purposes of distinguishing FAAWABAs from the rest of our gentle gender, I've invented a little checklist that will alert you to the dangers of getting caught in her snare or of becoming, yourself, the dreaded FAAWABA.

You see, one of the important goals of this guide is to identify the pamperable (of both sexes) as opposed to those Brothers and Sisters who will hurt you or take extreme advantage of you with a quickness.

Breaking a long code of silence, I am compelled, both as a writer and a recovering FAAWABA, to share some of her secrets.

TWENTY-FIVE CHARACTERISTICS OF A GENUINE FAAWABA

1. She can't listen; she's always complaining.
2. She can't be satisfied.
3. She never apologizes for being late but always blames you for being early.
4. She audits your time and charges you for hers.
5. She is happiest when you're miserable.
6. She gloats.
7. She rarely shows gratitude or appreciation for anything without a price tag.
8. She always compares the man she's with to her last husband, lover, or father.
9. She blames anyone (and everyone) for her problems and shortcomings.
10. She changes voices—depending on to whom she is speaking.
11. She is loud at inappropriate times.
12. She can't stand hearing another Sister's good news.
13. She holds grudges against others into the next millennium.
14. She answers your questions with a question.
15. She hates eating alone. She hates being alone.
16. She insults you in public; she hangs up on you in private.
17. She is passionate only about negative things.
18. She can't accept criticism, and she can't give praise.
19. She cries to excuse her bad behavior.
20. She makes fun of you or laughs at you.

21. While making love, she just lies there.
22. She fusses, cusses, and never discusses.
23. She sulks.
24. She is supercritical of everyone except herself.
25. She never washes clothes, changes the bedding, puts a cap on the toothpaste, or refills the paper-towel holder without an argument.

A genuine FAAWABA is totally self-centered and engrossed in her own performance. She doesn't give a hoot about anyone else.

[Why, this Sister wouldn't stomp on a grape wearing a pair of army boots—but she'll come to your party and drink all the wine.]

I've also noticed that typically, the FAAWABA in the nineties is into self-mutilation.

She wears twenty pounds of nylon braids woven tightly into her scalp, three-inch acrylic fingernails with rhinestones on her pinkie fingers, two pairs of humongous gold-plated pierced earrings, a diamond nose stud, and crippling four-inch red vinyl stiletto heels.

[Maybe it's the pain that makes her so mean.]

Now, I'll admit that most Sisters have a little FAAWABA mixed in their blood. In fact, every woman does, regardless of her race or background.

[This isn't about a breeding thing. FAAWABAs come in all flavors.]

I'm sure you know your share of *Ferocious Anglo-American Women with a Bad Attitude* or a few *Ferocious Asian-American Women with a Bad Attitude.* Or even some FHAWABAs—that's *Ferocious Hispanic-American Women with a Bad Attitude.*

But somehow, most people think that Sisters are the only ones who suffer from this madness. We're the ones who are getting all the fallout.

A White woman who has a bad day or acts outrageous is perceived as out of sorts or going through PMS. At her lowest, she is hysterical.

Black Sisters get no such break.

If we so much as raise an eyebrow, we are perceived as hysterical. When an otherwise mild-mannered Blackwoman gets her feathers ruffled, she is merely living *down* to expectations.

The FAAWABAs among us have given *all* Blackwomen a bad name. They have made it nearly impossible for any woman of color to have legitimate rage, lest her Blackman say, "Now there you go. You're acting just like a *Blackwoman*."

He doesn't mean you, Girlfriend. That's the *FAAWABA* he's talking about.

[He's only defensive because experience has taught him that the FAAWABA will break his heart in a beat.]

That is why I say let us unmask the dreaded FAAWABA and let the real Sisters shine.

OK, so I'm a little down on FAAWABAs. But let me explain why.

See, FAAWABAs have frequently gotten the best of me in matters of men, jobs, and the loyalties of other friends.

[They always seem to stand, or lie, in the way.]

One day I wondered why FAAWABAs seem to have every advantage. And privilege.

I mean, if there was a contest between a FAAWABA and a gentle Sister, the FAAWABA would show up late and still win.

Suddenly I realized that FAAWABAs make great bitches because they practice.

Gentle Sisters can't help it; they are gentle. They don't work at being real or kind or anything. It is almost impossible for a gentle Sister to be vengeful and mean.

FAAWABAs, on the other hand, work at their witchcraft until they have it perfected to a fine art.

A FAAWABA will make her man pay to see any one of her "Victoria's Secrets."

[No wonder many a great gal comes in second place.]

To tell the truth, I've never known a FAAWABA who wasn't good at picking a fight (on her turf or yours, but always on her own terms), embarrassing an intended victim, or leaving.

[This Sister will move in a minute.]

We may not understand the allure of this sepia femme fatale, but we've got to give her her propers. She's a tough act to beat and an even tougher act to follow.

You see, a FAAWABA captivates her man before she castrates him. Then she decapitates him.

After she's full and satisfied, his memory is nothing more than a belch.

[Have mercy!]

When a FAAWABA turns her man out, she'll throw his clothes in the street or she'll burn them. She'll charge him with assault or rape. She'll call his friends, his family, and his boss with her character assassinations.

If she's a friend of yours, count on her loyalty only when it's convenient—for her. FAAWABAs generally make lousy friends.

On the positive side of the balance sheet, it's good to know that if you are being victimized or brutalized by a FAAWABA—in friendship or in love—your choices are clear.

You can (a) leave (as in pack up and split) or (b) help her to see herself as she truly is.

If you choose the latter and you want to preserve your sanity, you must perform a *FAAWABAdectomy* as quickly as possible.

[I'm telling you, you've got to operate right away!]

A FAAWABAdectomy is *un*plastic surgery—that is, it's personality reconstruction by removing all the plastic.

Now, here's one five-step FAAWABAdectomy, a nonsurgical procedure that should stop the growth of the FAAWABA's negatron behavior. Without fuel, you see, her negativity should burn itself out in no time.

If you are a practicing FAAWABA or FHAWABA and have run off every man close to you, you may wish to perform a *Self-*

THE FIVE-STEP FAAWABADECTOMY

1. When she starts acting ugly, toss a mirror up in front of her face. This forces the FAAWABA to see herself as she really is.
2. Secretly tape-record the FAAWABA's next tirade, and spring it on her when she comes to you normal.
3. When she tries to bite your head off, throw her a dog biscuit.
4. Warn her that you're going to blow the whistle on her bad behavior. Every time she acts up, do just that. And blow it loud.
5. Reward her for each day of good behavior with a little treat. If she makes it through an entire week without an outburst, make it a big treat.

FAAWABAdectomy. You can put yourself under, just like with self-hypnosis.

Sure, it's a little more difficult to operate on yourself, but it is possible for you to relax and get inside your head. Become aware of what you are thinking, how you are behaving, and how others are perceiving you.

[If you find you are still barking to get attention and still cursing your blessings, my Sister, the procedure didn't work. I recommend that you try it again, or get some professional help.]

Just think, all the power you have given to creating evil you can give to creating joy. I promise you, it is a better trip to make people smile than to make them cry.

If your goal is to have a Blackman beating a path to your door, begging to be pampered and to pamper you, teach the FAAWABA side of your personality some control. Take her to finishing school. Form a twelve-step recovery group with other admitted FAAWABAs. Check your FAAWABA coat of arms at the door.

Every Sister has the capacity to turn the FAAWABA inside her into a WAAWABA. That's *Wonderful African-American Woman with a Bright Attitude.* If only she will learn to give a little, bend a little, and share a lot.

11 WAAWABAS IN YOUR MIDST

I've noticed that men don't put nearly enough emphasis on finding, dating, or marrying a lady with a good attitude and manners to match.

I've heard some Brothers say they are settling for good looks and good sex because they don't believe they can find a woman of quality, intelligence, grace, beauty, and sex appeal all in one package.

[Men believe that such a creature, like the fabled unicorn, doesn't exist.]

The Sister I'm talking about can hold down a full-time job, cook a warm meal from scratch, balance a checkbook, maintain a sterling credit rating, serve as president of the PTA, keep her looks up, and keep a clean house—all without complaining.

Not only do such women exist but they are the Great Unnoticed of our species.

I'm convinced that these resilient Sisters can do almost anything they set their minds to. About the only thing they can't seem to do in the nineties is attract a good Blackman.

For the sake of balance, as we explore the pleasures of pampering, I want to tell my Brothers that these thrifty and thoughtful Sisters are one of America's great untapped natural resources that is still not available for export.

[These ladies are still holding out to be discovered by the Homeboys at home.]

I call these underrated Sisters the W.A.A.W.A.B.A.s—that's Wonderful African-American Women with a Bright Attitude, or *WABs,* for short, and there are thousands of them!

In fact, as they roam the continent in search of the endangered Good Blackman, their numbers are growing like the Mongol tribes of ancient Asia.

Like the *Nice Guy,* this gal rarely nabs a nod from the opposite sex. She is too *nice* to be interesting. She is too down-to-earth to be exciting. She is too wholesome to be sexy. Her appeal doesn't hold a candle to the torch Homeboy is carrying for her FAAWABA Sister.

From coast to coast I hear a sad WAB's Lament, like the slow plaintive moans of a chain gang; filled with woeness, these Sisters seem resigned to lifelong loneliness:

I've given up my anger,
I've put away my rage.
I don't want to treat no man
Like a bird in a gilded cage.
I'm cute, I'm smart, I'm sexy,
I don't scream or shout.
So why does every Brother out there
Want to dog me out?

I am sure that this low lament, like an out-of-range dog whistle, isn't even heard by most good Black Brothers. And many men have admitted to me that they were, in fact, on their way to the arms of the gentle WAB when they were unfortunately sidetracked by the dreaded FAAWABA.

[Guys just don't get it. Everywhere I go, I preach that a FAAWABA—that slithering, sidewinder type of Sister—is dangerous to a man's health.]

If a Brother wants to live a long and productive life, he should take some advice from over half of the U.S. prison population and two-thirds of all homeless men: a FAAWABA is not a Brother's answer to eternal bliss.

[And chances are, if Homeboy is honest, the sex ain't even that great.]

Some hapless Brothers are courting danger and don't even know it. A FAAWABA will often disguise herself as a WAB before she moves in, becomes engaged, or has her first baby. But by then, it's too late—she's trapped her man.

[If a Brother is on the fast track to anywhere, a FAAWABA is his most deadly detour.]

A young widower friend of mine, left alone to raise his five-year-old daughter, was dating a beautiful WABish Sister who owned a day-care center and adored children.

[This gentle Girlfriend loved pampering her relationships.]

Along comes his cutie-pie former college sweetheart—now a young mother herself, trapped in a loveless marriage with one of the city's wealthiest men—and she wants to fool around.

[This guzzling Girlfriend loved pandering her relationships.]

Three months into the pant-and-groan affair—shortly after Brother-Man ran out of motel money and credit cards for their clandestine meetings at the beach, Unhappy Married Lady became fascinated with an NFL football star who was tossing a little pig iron her way.

[Was my friend benched, or what?]

I've heard hundreds of these WABs-in-disguise stories. Like any human tragedy, each one is different, but they all share the same sorrow-filled endings.

[See chapter 15, "Overlove."]

Little do most men realize, a FAAWABA lurks in the shadows of every healthy relationship, ready to ruin, ravage, and wreck the heck out of it.

[Like a puppy with a slipper, this woman has no respect.]

I hope this chapter will be a wake-up call for the Brotherhood.

Good Brothers don't have to be a FAAWABA's foil. If our good Blackmen will but open their eyes, they'll see that WABs are everywhere.

Gentle WABs can be found coaching kiddie sports, updating their job skills in a continuing education class, or shopping (for groceries, rarely clothes).

You'll find them in libraries and bookstores, Laundromats and dry-cleaning establishments. They frequent schools, seminars, and self-help groups. They are active in sports and have a penchant for art. They give of their time and their energy to charities, churches, and the community.

[The WABish Sisters I know are confounded when Brothers say they can't find a good Blackwoman.]

As a four-star Master Pamperer, I have a public-spirited duty to defeat my sinister FAAWABA Sisters and exalt their all-too-quiet and maligned counterpart—the gentle, often docile, non-threatening, smiling WAB—a woman who will unquestionably make the best wife, the best business partner, and the best friend a man could ever hope for.

[A WAB is not perfect. She might drop a few stitches from time to time. She might drop her guard now and then. She may drop the ball or even drop a hint. The only thing this Sistah won't do is drop her standards.]

In spite of a FAAWABA's many clever disguises, there is now a no-fail personality test to help Brothers identify a true Wonderful African-American Woman with a Bright Attitude.

This amazingly simple test can be administered to Anglo, Asian, or Hispanic Sisters with the same revealing results.

THE WABOMETER DETECTION TEST

1. If your man is working in the mail room (or another entry-level job), you
   a. want him to turn to crime.
   b. tolerate him.
   c. pack his lunch.

2. If your Blackman just lost his job, you
   a. turn to his best friend for comfort.
   b. feel sorry for yourself.
   c. help him update his résumé.
3. If he treats you like a queen, but your girlfriends call him a dork, you
   a. make fun of him.
   b. keep him out of their sight.
   c. turn a deaf ear to your friends.
4. If you are dating a man who still lives at home with his parents, you
   a. insist that he get his own spot.
   b. put one hundred dollars down on a bachelor pad and hand him the rent papers.
   c. frequently visit because you feel comfortable with his folks.
5. If your husband wants to go back to school or learn a trade, you
   a. put him down for entertaining a midlife career move.
   b. remind him how good his job is.
   c. help him fill out the applications.
6. If your fiancé wants to start a business instead of have a big wedding, you
   a. tell him the money for your dress is nonrefundable.
   b. get pregnant and rush the wedding.
   c. take your laptop to Las Vegas and help him write the business plan.
7. If you just moved in with a man who wants to spend time with his kids (by a previous marriage) or invite his elderly parents for a visit, you
   a. go O-F-F.
   b. get sick.
   c. help him to fix up the spare bedroom.
8. If your lover, who is into "natural" beauty, gives you $250 for a makeover, you
   a. spend $250 for a day at the salon getting four-inch acrylic fingernails, eighteen-inch hair extensions, and eyebrow electrolysis.

b. spend $150 at the salon on two-inch acrylic fingernails and a hair weave and $100 for a new outfit.

c. spend $75 at the salon getting a sassy hair bob, a manicure and pedicure, buy a sexy little number on sale for $50, and put $125 in the bank.

9. If your main squeeze wants to stay home on Saturday night, you

a. pout until he agrees to take you out.

b. invite seven of your girlfriends over for a whist party.

c. ask him what movie he'd like to rent from the video store.

10. If you see your new male companion talking with another woman, you

a. ask him if he's fooling around.

b. start checking his pockets.

c. assume that the relationship is innocent.

With the "WABometer Detection Test," there is only one right answer for the true WAAWABA in your midst.

So how do you think you scored, Girlfriend? What kind of woman are you?

If you answered *c* to every question, you have passed the WABometer Detection Test with flying colors. You should be proud.

If you answered *a* or *b* to any of the ten questions, dear Sister, you flunked the WABometer Detection Test, and we've got some more work to do.

[With this test, there is no middle ground. Either you are or you aren't.]

Now, let's say that you are a Sister who has passed the WABometer Detection Test and still you have no Brothers beating down your door.

[He's too busy sniffin' around that snake hole.]

If getting bit is his bag, please make out a living trust for his next of kin, his favorite charity, and make yourself—as his trusted friend—the executor of his estate.

[That is, if he has anything left to split among his survivors after the FAAWABA is through with him.]

If, however, you are acquainted with some reasonably sane Brother with the intelligence God gave a rock; if you know a man who doesn't like a whole lot of grief with his gusto or pain in his passion; if you know a Brother who is not into pathological relationships, it is your WABish duty to point out the very distinctive differences between you and your FAAWABA Sister.

[The word up is that a WAB is like Maalox to a machinist—she'll settle your nerves in a gulp.]

I am pleased to report that there is now an organized effort to stop the FAAWABA onslaught. I understand that some WAAWABAs today are fighting back with a weapon of their own—a "WAAWABA Characteristics List." Taking pride in their militant niceness, these WABs with an attitude are now circulating their membership qualifications through E-mail, voice mail, and regular mail to every Brother who can read or will listen.

These nameless Nubian guerrilla WABs remind Brothers that they are a tribe with unique qualities, traits, and idiosyncrasies common only to their clan.

They challenge Brothers to observe them in their own habitat—relaxing at home, driving to work, on the phone with their girlfriends, or out on the town.

If a Brother has a genuine WAAWABA in his midst, chances are she also

1. says "please."
2. says "thank you."
3. means what she says.
4. doesn't gossip.
5. offers to help.
6. is sincere.
7. is monogamous.
8. is passionate about positive things.
9. remembers to pay her debts.
10. listens.

11. sleeps well at night.
12. smiles.
13. laughs.
14. is a good friend.
15. is a good neighbor.
16. is trustworthy.
17. returns borrowed things.
18. shares credit.
19. accepts responsibility.
20. has a warm handshake.
21. looks you in the eye when she's speaking.
22. likes surprises.
23. is proud of how old she is.
24. is not verbally abusive.
25. respects nature.
26. honors elders.
27. cherishes children.
28. leaves a tip.
29. thanks the cook.
30. is open to suggestions.
31. has empathy for others.
32. doesn't hold grudges.
33. is reasonable.
34. always pulls her car up to the first gas pump.
35. is a courteous driver.
36. doesn't hog the basket in the Laundromat.
37. won't embarrass you.
38. turns off lights.
39. recycles.
40. enjoys happy endings.
41. likes sports.
42. changes the toilet paper roll.
43. refills the juice pitcher.
44. signs contracts.
45. shares the remote control.
46. lets someone in the grocery line with only three items go first.

47. doesn't waste food.
48. doesn't waste time.
49. returns your phone calls.
50. is a good cook.

[Now does this Sister deserve positive attention, or what?]

I am encouraged that there are still plenty of Ms. Rights out there who have good jobs and good credit, women who don't do drugs or worship the devil, Sisters who don't live with nine kids by different fathers in a house full of crazy relatives.

If you won't take my word for it, just ask any of the thousands of smiling men I've spoken with all over the country.

Interview your singing neighbor—the one who's been happily married for twenty-five years. Take your coworker to coffee—the one who shares *everything* with his wife. Ask your buddy whom everyone teases but he does as he pleases *with* his ol' lady.

To a man, any Brother who is spending serious time with a WAAWABA will tell you that he has struck gold.

[I'm talkin' royalty here, boys. Queens, princesses, and noble ladies who deserve to be pampered.]

One executive Brother who admits that he is totally satisfied with his wife of sixteen years told me about his wild bachelor days in the marines. "The only reason I'm alive today," he said, "is because I met and married my wife.

"I was a marine who landed in a brothel in every port," he explained. "My wife was the only good girl I couldn't get."

[Don't tell me that "Want What You Can't Have" game still works?]

This handsome hombre explained to a group of rapt young men how his life changed in a single fateful weekend.

"I got four back-to-back phone calls," he said. "The first call came from a Sister in Philadelphia who charged me with getting her pregnant; the second was from a jealous husband in San Diego who checked his long-distance phone bill and threatened to blow me away; a third came in from Hawaii, a marine buddy of mine told me that he'd tested HIV-positive. And the last call was from my mother, who wanted me to fly home right away because my father had had a stroke."

This good Black Brother says that he's often ridiculed by his lascivious and wolf-whiffing peers for pampering his lady. These are Brothers, he says, who either never go home or don't have a home to go to.

[I know a lot of guys who think that *Disclosure* is a Disney movie.]

"I love going home to my woman," he says. "Home is definitely where my heart is."

To the loud chagrin of the Brothers who wanted to goad this proud Blackman into an argument, Homeboy had to split. He was on his way home to his WAB wife and two kids. While they shouted him down with their desperate taunts, the good Black Brother just shrugged and sauntered calmly out the door.

"Y'all are just loud to mask the lonely," he laughed. "I just hope the good Lord lets you young Brothers stick around long enough to learn that it takes a quiet woman to calm a desperate man."

12 ONE HUNDRED AND TWO WAYS TO PAMPER YOUR BLACKWOMAN

These days everyone I know is riding waves of uncertainty. I have friends who are either trying to swim through a difficult relationship or they are jumping ship. Some are trying to stay afloat financially, and many are going under. I've got several girlfriends who are swimming in a sea of self-pity and drowning in depression.

Everyone, it seems, is looking for a lifeboat and sending up SOS flares like crazy.

Now I'm no navy admiral, but if you can answer someone's distress call in stormy waters, saving a Brother from shipwrecking himself, well, Girlfriend, you've earned my Himpressions Medal of Sheroism.

Any Sister who got anything out of chapter 7, "One Hundred and One Ways to Pamper Your Blackman" is my shero. For in devoting effort and energy to building a relationship with a Blackman instead of tearing it down, you have proved yourself an exceptional champion.

I want you to know, Girlfriend, you are in good company.

We've got a lot of sheroes. Sisters like Whitney Houston, Cookie Johnson, Felicia Moon, and Oprah Winfrey have stood in the public's glare with total calm—and in total support of their Blackmen.

Since my "101" list was published in 1993, it has become obvious to me that there are many Sisters who have taken a hankering to pampering.

These are women with the unflappable belief that if they are blessed to be seaworthy, their search-and-rescue missions will eventually lead them to a Treasure Island.

[I mean, if you've got a "nice" Brother with a job who wants to build you a generator, go to church with you on Sunday, and is willing to take an AIDS test before you make love, I think he's worth some consideration.]

[Thank God, today there are WAAWABAs in our midst!]

Now, I've promised my shero Sisters that there are sweet rewards awaiting you for taking this hard line on pampering your Blackman.

I've assured my WAAWABA Sisters that if they will simply throw out a little more rope to our seasick Brothers—initiating some pampering in their relationships—most right-minded Brothers will take the hint and follow suit.

[You got it, Girlfriend, I'm talkin' 'bout Pampering Partnerships here!]

I'll be the first to admit that many Brothers have never encountered a WAB and therefore don't know how to treat her.

[Before Dr. Charles Drew formulated plasma, no one knew what to do with raw blood products either.]

The point is, a Blackman has to know how to manage a woman who is as rare and wonderful as the gentle WAAWABA.

So, by popular request, after two more years of exhaustive research, for Brothers who have a sense of their good fortune and may not know how to handle it, and for those subtle Sisters who have graciously shared their turn-ons with me, here are 102 tried and tested ways to pamper your Blackwoman.

1. Speak highly of her to others.
2. Teach her new things about life.
3. Show and tell her you love her daily.
4. Make a card for her with your own sweet words.
5. Take her dancing under the stars.
6. Make lunch dates.
7. Give her a facial.
8. Bring flowers to her on the job.
9. Pay her to skip work, and take her on a picnic.
10. Treat her to a pedicure.
11. Meet her for a blind date.
12. Rub her feet at the end of the day.
13. Buy her a just-because gift.
14. Prepare a gourmet dinner, serve it to her, and wash the dishes.
15. Make love to her without entering her.
16. Take her to a play or a ballet.
17. Give her a heated-oil body massage.
18. Brush her hair before she goes to bed.
19. Shampoo her hair for her.
20. Make her your best friend.
21. Put the toilet seat down.
22. Don't think she can read your mind.
23. Be soft and gentle with her.
24. Talk to her; don't holler at her.
25. Work on a project together.
26. Write a poem for her.
27. Read to her at night.
28. Read a book together.
29. Study the Bible together.
30. Instead of the boys' night out, make it your woman's night out.
31. Let her model the outfit you will buy her.
32. Make her "Queen for a Day."
33. Have a sportsless weekend.
34. Learn a foreign language together.
35. Know her favorite colors.
36. Keep her shoe size, dress size, and ring size on hand.
37. Buy her a lovely perfume.

38. Prepare her favorite meal for her.
39. Keep the honey in your honeymoon.
40. Mean what you say and say what you mean.
41. Treat her like your queen.
42. Open doors for her.
43. Send her a singing telegram at work.
44. Run a bubble bath for her.
45. Wash her back.
46. Pick up her clothes from the cleaners.
47. Take her shoes for shine and repair.
48. Go horseback riding together.
49. Plant a rosebush and maintain it in her honor.
50. Be faithful to her at all times.
51. Be nice to her family.
52. Don't hit on her girlfriends.
53. Make an audiotape of her favorite music.
54. Stay in good physical condition for her.
55. Help in the kitchen.
56. Mail her an invitation.
57. Spoon-feed her dessert.
58. Make the bed after you've made love, while she's in the shower.
59. Play love games.
60. Be honest.
61. Make short- and long-range goals together.
62. Don't fool around.
63. Be supportive and show appreciation.
64. Have scented candles lit throughout the house, and wait for her on a bed of flower petals.
65. Never go to bed angry.
66. Kiss and make up.
67. Name a star after her.
68. Compliment her on her cooking.
69. Don't make her feel foolish or embarrass her in public.
70. Be dependable.
71. Never curse her.
72. Treat her like a lady.

73. Never compare her to anyone.
74. Have faith in her.
75. Keep your promises.
76. Clean the house (or pay someone to do it).
77. Pick up (your clothes) after yourself.
78. Volunteer before she asks you to do something.
79. Sing to her.
80. Hold hands.
81. When the lights go down, put your arm around her in the movie theater, at a concert, or at a play.
82. Compliment what's new about her.
83. Keep her car tuned and in good running order.
84. Remember her birthday.
85. Remember your anniversary.
86. When making love, be gentle.
87. Be respectful of her parents.
88. Enjoy her company.
89. Take a class together.
90. Praise her to her children.
91. Praise her to her parents; praise her to your parents.
92. Bring your money home.
93. Don't constantly bring up the past.
94. Attend church services with her.
95. Be an accomplished lover.
96. From time to time, do the laundry.
97. Ask her how her day went, and take a real interest in her answer.
98. Call to let her know you're going to be late.
99. Kiss her hello and good-bye.
100. Give her undivided attention when she needs you to listen.
101. Say "please" and "thank you."
102. Be as one.

13 INTERVIEW WITH AN OLD O.G.

Please understand me, Girlfriend: when I set about the task of writing a guide on pampering the Blackman for Sisters, I didn't just talk to wonderful, together Brothers who are looking for an African-American Queen to fulfill their dreams.

One of my friends, an older gentleman, is a retired Original Gangster (an Old O.G.) who is not behind bars. This in itself is a major accomplishment that earns him a lot of respect.

[Any Old Original Gangster who lives long enough to retire from criminal activities is, for a writer, prime topsoil in the garden of ideas.]

You might be surprised to know that this fifty-year-old former gangster today lives a genteel life: he is as fatherly as Sinbad, as grandfatherly as Bill Cosby; he is a respected businessman, an athlete, gourmet cook, and a life scholar.

Little would one suspect that a Blackman with so many assets was once a menace to society—with a number of felony convictions, years behind bars, and a trail of broke and broken-hearted women in his wake.

As a researcher of the highest intent, I thought it might be instructive to the Sisterhood to get a take on the underbelly of pampering the Blackman, from a rehabilitated scoundrel and admitted former con artist.

[Some people think that an interview with a vampire is an interesting trip. Try an interview with an Old O.G. for a really surreal reality check.]

It hit me that most Sisters I know—present company included—have only been victimized by such wild men. Rarely do we have an opportunity to study them objectively.

[Maybe if we study a dog or two, we won't get bitten.]

WARNING: The following interview may not be suitable for minors. Parental discretion is advised.

V.S.: How long have you been an Original Gangster?

Old O.G.: I am not an Original Gangster; I'm an *Old* Original Gangster! An O.G. is a young cat who is still trying to earn a reputation. He talks crazy and takes crazy chances. An Old O.G., if he's smart, has learned that lyin' and crime don't pay.

V.S.: How long were you an active member of the criminal community? And why did you retire from the life [of crime]?

Old O.G.: I was in and out of jail from the time I was twenty-one, always trying to get something for nothing. I missed my children growing up, but I've been given a second chance with my grandkids, and I'm not going to blow it. Having matured, I realize that I am blessed to be alive and free, and I have a valuable contribution to make to society.

V.S.: Did your wife know that you were engaged in criminal activities?

Old O.G.: I've been married four times, and all of my wives knew that when I wasn't working a square nine-to-five, I was doing crime. Of course. How else could we afford giant-screen television sets, expensive cars, and private schools for the kids?

V.S.: Who didn't know that you were engaged in crime?

Old O.G.: I don't think my kids knew that I was a criminal when they were growing up. When I was in jail, their mothers would tell them that Daddy was in the military or the space program or something like that.

Most of my outside women didn't know that I had a double life. They just thought I was a mysterious kind of guy, like a Shaft or a Black James Bond.

V.S.: What kind of men did you meet in jail?

Old O.G.: Women who've never visited a joint would be surprised to find a campus full of the most attractive, likable Brothers of intelligence on the planet. All behind bars. If you're wondering where all the Blackmen are, just check out any state or federal institution.

V.S.: Well, what's wrong with a Sister hooking up with a Brother who has done some time?

Old O.G.: It all depends on what the Brother did time for. A woman should ask a lot of questions. If it was a crime of violence . . . well, he had best have gotten some help with his problems. If it was drug related, he's going to need two jobs to keep himself occupied and away from old friends and bad habits.

In any case, Homeboy has to want to go straight. You can lead the horse to water, but you can't make him drink it.

V.S.: Why does it appear that some women are attracted to con men and turned off by "nice" guys?

Old O.G.: Women looking for a Prince Charming are attracted to a man who seems to have everything. A con artist always looks like he makes six figures, even if he's just gotten out of jail and is on General Relief.

He's bronze, handsome, and buffed. (That's the benefit he got from walkin' the yard at Riker's Island for six years.) He's very well spoken, intelligent, and up on current events. (Most penitentiaries have Toastmasters, study clubs, cultural awareness programs, and libraries.) He doesn't do drugs. (Urine testing takes place every month while he's on parole.) He is a quiet man who doesn't have many friends. (Most of them are still in lockup.)

He is neat (he had to keep his cell military-clean); he cooks (after working in the mess hall for five years) and even irons (regulation creases are required in those prison grays). He goes to church. (That's one of the best places to meet a Square Jane.) And he loves his mother. (After all, he hasn't seen her in twelve years.)

Now here is a man, from all outward appearances, who looks like a good catch, but if you scratch just one layer below the surface, you may find a Brother with less than honorable intentions.

V.S.: If an O.G. has not changed his ways, how can a woman tell he is still involved in crime?

Old O.G.: He's got all day to play, an inexhaustible supply of money, and three or four ready explanations on why he's never settled down. His reasons are so good that you won't be tempted to ask too many more questions. His goal is to win your confidence; that's why they call him a confidence man.

V.S.: What lines does a con man use to attract a Sister's interest?

Old O.G.: To get her immediate interest, he might tell her that he's a former defensive end for the NFL, out on waivers, or an injured stock-car racer. He could say that he's a retired teamster, a retired navy man, or a musician with Earth, Wind, and Fire. He might be a firefighter out on disability, or say that he just came from Minnesota, where he sold his family's farm (after his father died).

If he's hitting on an intellectual Sister, he might say that he's a U.N. peacekeeper on assignment in Haiti. If he's rappin' to one of those silk-and-suede broads, he'll say that he's into real estate, with investments in Hawaii and Arizona.

Then there are some good sympathy moves—he's a widower, a single father who doesn't have custody of the kids (but wishes he did), or a guy whose wife just left him for a woman.

V.S.: Where does a con artist go to pick up a patsy?

Old O.G.: A good con doesn't hang out in bars, contrary to public opinion. A bad con does, because he's probably an alcoholic and any woman will do.

A real O.G. doesn't lurk in dark corners like in the movies. He's out there on the make, trying to attract a Sister of substance. So he goes where the Sisters of substance go: art and fashion shows, the gym, the beach, church socials, cruises, ski trips, and jazz concerts—almost anywhere you find good-looking solid dames, you'll find plenty of Original Gangsters playing games.

V.S.: What does an O.G. say to a Sister that a straight-up Brother won't?

Old O.G.: An O.G. who is running game on a broad never argues. He'll go along with almost any program. You are always beautiful. He'll never leave you. You don't have to keep a clean house. And you don't have to cook. The only thing he asks . . . the only thing he wants . . . and the only thing he insists on is that he manage your money.

V.S.: Have you used women?

Old O.G.: Of course. Some women ask to be used.

V.S.: Excuse me, Mr. Old O.G., how could you say such a thing? What do you mean, "some women ask to be used"?

Old O.G.: When a Sister flashes her Gold Cards or tries to impress a total stranger with how much she has, it sends a clear signal to any self-respecting O.G. that the market is open for trading.

V.S.: Does a Brother who uses women feel guilty?

Old O.G.: Nope.

V.S.: Are you advising Sisters to stay away from a Brother who looks too good to be true?

Old O.G.: Women make the mistake of underrating a plain man, a serious Brother who will be there in spite of the fact that he doesn't bring home six figures. Instead, she is looking for a man who fulfills her every fantasy. Too many soap operas, I think.

To me, a woman is an investment to a Brother. A Brother with righteous intentions thinks of his woman as his first and most important investment. He'll do anything to cherish and protect it.

An O.G. is a player who has invested in many women, and he's got to watch all of his investments—watch them or turn them over. He's not going to give away anything. See, a man who knows how to make his money always knows how to keep his money.

V.S.: How can a woman protect herself from being scammed by an O.G., con artist, or player?

Old O.G.: For one thing, if you try too hard to avoid it and run smack into a con . . .

V.S.: Sort of like the Ethiopian proverb that says, "She who runs from the red ant stumbles upon the stinging ant"?

Old O.G.: Exactly. A Sister thinks she is keeping company with a diamond, but flashy Homeboy is only a cubic zirconia. A real diamond has got a little dirt on it, and you got to dig. Too many Sisters these days don't want to dig for a relationship.

V.S.: Do you have any advice for a Sister who doesn't want to get her hands dirty?

Old O.G.: That kind of Sister is definite con bait. She is going to get sprung by a player because he's the only one who can stand her finicky ways.

V.S.: If you could offer one piece of wisdom that would enlighten millions of Sisters about the type of Brothers we should consider as matrimony material, what would it be?

Old O.G.: Don't judge a book by its cover.

V.S.: That's it?

Old O.G.: That's it!

V.S.: What would your Homeboys, the other Old Original Gangsters, say if they knew you were conducting this interview?

O.G.: They would definitely retire me.

V.S.: Thank you.

14 LOSS AND THE LOVING VOID

People who try to hold on to their worldly goods in the face of a natural disaster usually become casualties of that disaster.

Like a very wealthy man I once knew who tried to cheat death by not writing a will. His only instruction was that he be buried beside his beloved mother in the family plot.

Well, when he died, his ex-wife and the children made sure that his body was cremated.

[It just goes to show you.]

The idea that we can hold on to material things is ridiculous. The idea that we can hold on to a man is preposterous too. Everything passes and everything must change.

Everything.

The past is where it belongs—behind us.

My friend J. T. O'Hara always reminds me, "Yesterday is history. Tomorrow is a mystery. Today is the gift, and that's why they call it the present."

If we use the experiences of the past to make us wiser, we learn to appreciate the joy of a moment without trying to squeeze eternity out of it.

Holding is not having.

No one belongs to us. You can squeeze the life out of a relationship or smother it to death by not allowing it to breathe.

All living things need air, water, and room to grow.

Speaking of holding on, you can lose control of your relationship and spoil even the best thing with a trek through the painful pages of the past—his or yours.

You can't rewrite history. His story and your story—it's all history!

If I had a dollar for every woman I've met who has been hurt or lied to, I'd hold the keys to Atlantic City. The same applies to my good Brothers. We've all been down that road.

Further, in addition to being victims, most of us have been the victimizers.

OK, maybe not yesterday. But remember that super-nice guy, the smart one who helped you with your freshman algebra?

How many dates did you break with him after the football star hinted that he *might* be free Saturday night?

[Hello!]

Oh, yes, we've all been the marksmen as well as the incidental target.

[Remember chapter 5, "Nice"?]

Seasons of promiscuity, chronic bad behaviors, sending out killer negatron bombs—blowing up at everyone for nothing—oh, yes, we've all gone through phases that we're less than proud of.

[So what else is new? Now, who's going to throw that first stone?]

It is amazing to me how much present time we dedicate to the past.

We're not going to spend any time on war stories here. They are just too gruesome—and far too repetitious.

[But if you've just got to go for the gore, check out chapter 15, "Overlove."]

All I want to say is, if you're living in the past, how on earth can you enjoy the present?

Enjoy the moment. Treasure the memory, and when it's over . . . Well, that's coming up too!

Learn to turn the page.

The risk of loving is losing. For every victor there are a thousand losers.

You diss one man and get your heart broken by the next five. That's life.

Let's face it—the odds are against all of us.

So why fall in love in the first place, when we can almost be certain that it will result in pain?

Because if we try long enough, with all our hearts, we may win. Certainly over time the odds will improve, and we will win enough victories to last a lifetime.

Love is always worth your trouble.

The most profound hurt I've experienced once brought me the most exquisite pleasure.

Drawing pleasure out of a memory of love is far richer than the mundane absence of it.

Can you count the times you've been in love? OK, infatuated will do.

I've been infatuated hundreds of times and in love—I mean that hope-to-die love thing—over a dozen times. Each one, in his time, was the love of my life. And it was true—at that time.

When I look back through the years, I am grateful to each of my adored. Just by giving, I received so much more.

[Love is the answer. No matter what the question is.]

One husband introduced me to the world of business, as my role was to manage the family finances.

One lover gave me the gift of self-confidence.

[I learned to stand up to him.]

Another Brother—who didn't stick around long enough to find out how much I cared for him—invited me to verbalize my ambition. He helped me to realize that I could accomplish anything.

I was a willing and able student, but in those early days, when the breakup came, most of the men I've loved thought my high drama was an expression of my low self-esteem.

Sure, I regret the dramatic scenes I created, although I do confess, I've never shed a tear I didn't grow from.

[If you've got a speck of dirt in your eye, you are either

going to cry it out or wash it out. Either way, you are cleansing your injury.]

Tears, it seems to me, are healthy expressions of loss. Wallowing in them, however, will drown you.

The first step in getting over an old hurt is to embrace the loss as a lesson. So you got burned. Lesson learned.

The only time you are not learning something new—about yourself and what you're attracting to your life—is when you get stuck in the past and are constantly trying to re-create it.

Speculation is pure recreation. The old what-if game.

What if he wasn't married? What if he wasn't gay? What if he wasn't so jealous? What if he wasn't on drugs?

[Was it a misperception that made you think he was such a nice guy? Was it a *dis*perception that made him take such extreme advantage of you?]

I know how you feel. We've all been down that bumpy road of speculation. Let me assure you, some questions that take a moment to ask may not be answered in your lifetime.

When we dig our way into the speculation rut, we can't get out of it. So we get comfortable with the pain. It becomes familiar.

We become so used to life's potholes that we forget the damage they're doing to our tires.

We seem to hold on to the horrors of lost loves like war medals—bringing them out of their gilded little boxes like trophies of misery.

And please don't think that perpetual heartache doesn't manifest itself in every aspect of your life. I see women every day who are zombies of their own making, slaves to loss and rejection. They can't get over the pain. As a consequence, they can't get over.

Behind the translucent veneer of chic togetherness is the stonelike facade of a woman scorned. I don't care what this Sister is wearing, you can see through to her anger like glass.

[Now, you know what they say about a scorned woman. No man in his right mind buys a one-way ticket for a vacation in hell.]

All I'm saying, Girlfriend, is that everyone has a past. But no one is doomed to repeat it in perpetuity. This is not *The Twilight Zone.*

[It's OK to idle, my Sistah—just don't turn yourself off.]

The price you pay for loving deeply is hurting much. There is no getting around it. But don't let that hurt shut down your emotional power plant. The only way you can accept a new love is to let go of the old hurts.

[As with any form of energy, you've got to expel the poisonous gas.]

I always used to be in love with a man. I was a magnet for love. My love life was like a trapeze act—swinging from one relationship to another, with a few seconds of suspended hurt in between.

When you are falling out of love, I've found that there is usually a *Loving Void* that you've got to go through.

A Loving Void is the space between the old relationship you are leaving and the new one you have yet to discover.

You know, like cleaning out your garage: there is always an emptiness that accompanies clearing out the old junk in your life.

It's tempting to fill the Loving Void with the first man who rings your bell.

[Like buying up everything you see at the first garage sale you come across.]

Please resist the temptation. You're not ready for anything except healing.

To heal yourself, to prepare for the healthy relationship you truly deserve, you've got to go to work.

I believe in self-help—self-anything you can do to get better.

Take a class, get active in an exercise program or a sport. Try a new look, a new haircut. Move. Redecorate. Help the homeless. Or the elderly. Join a church or a civic group. Develop an interest outside your problems.

Do something positive for yourself and for others.

You'll be so busy, so entertained, and so proud of yourself that you'll hardly notice time passing.

[With your insight being nourished, your outsight can't help but grow too.]

Staying busy, filling your time with nurturing activities, will naturally make you a more interesting person and a more attractive person to be around.

Learn to appreciate your loss and the Loving Void like the silence in a still night.

If you'll listen with a keen ear and an open mind, I'm sure you'll discover that there is peace in the void.

In fact, there is nothing like a little Loving Void to give you a sense of your own bliss.

Some time ago I wrote a little thank-you poem to a man with whom I was destined to share only one wonderful weekend. I hope it puts this loss thing in a little clearer perspective.

People come,
Some stay,
Some pass.
Not everything is made to last.
Sometimes the best
Is just a little treat.
It doesn't hang around long,
But it sure is sweet.

15 OVERLOVE

I come unglued like a pair of cheap shoes when a Sister tells me that she pampered a Blackman once and he took advantage of her.

Let me assure you that *pampering* and *abuse* don't even belong in the same sentence together.

My simple advice is, be careful whom you pamper—he just might like it enough to stick around.

[You may think that he's falling in love, but he's really falling in obsession.]

Maybe there wouldn't be all this confusion if someone would just write a song about that human condition that goes well beyond love into the outer limits of human emotions.

I call it *overlove*.

You know, like overdrive, overindulge, overspend, overpower, overreact, or over-anything. Too much of a good thing will make a body hurt himself.

Eating will keep you alive; overeating will make you obese. Cooked food is warm and nourishing; an overcooked meal will make you sick. Exposure to the sun will give you a healthy glow; overexposure will give you skin cancer. Parents who protect their children are nurturing. Parents who overprotect their kids are smothering.

Overlove is love to the max.

[A pot of boiling love spilling over.]

Like all the other *overs,* overlove is a total waste. It's love that will just get so worked up and smoky that it will either all evaporate or explode.

Overlove will drive a rich man to the poorhouse. It'll make a bus operator drive into a ditch and turn a schoolteacher into a prostitute. It'll make a preacher leave the pulpit. It'll make a welder lose his grip. It'll turn a doctor into a druggie and a nurse into a syringe-wielding psychopath.

Overlove is that condition that will make an otherwise sane person go crazy.

Through a sea of tears and heartbreak, its destination is always disaster. It has no positive redemptive value and has an afterlife of at least forty years. Once you're hooked, you're sunk. That's overlove.

I'm convinced that *love* has gotten a bad rap because of *overlove.* People think that love makes them behave badly, kill someone, or seek revenge on a national TV talk show. Let's get that straight: that's not *love.*

Love is pure. It is kind and giving and forgiving. Love is when you wish someone the best, regardless of what's in it for you.

If love is a puppy, overlove is a ravenous full-grown Doberman pinscher. If love is a tingle, overlove is electrocution. If love is a gentle stream, overlove is Niagara Falls.

When you ponder the worst for someone you're close to or when you know that they have similar designs on you—well, that's overlove.

When you'd hurt yourself just to hurt someone else—that's overlove.

[Overlove is like living on a roller coaster. You just gotta learn to eat your hot dog and sleep through the bumpy ride.]

The most notorious overlover I can think of in the nineties is O. J. Simpson. Like President Kennedy's assassination, we may never know the full truth about O. J.'s involvement in the tragic double murders of Nicole Brown Simpson and Ron Goldman. But it's pretty clear that O. J. was on overlove during the fateful summer of '94.

Overlovin' is not just a male thing. I figure that Susan Smith had a pretty tragic case of it too.

[And remember *Fatal Attraction*? Let's face it, there are definitely a few of us who will try to fry a guy.]

In truth, we all know our share of people in obviously toxic relationships who are in the throes of this dangerous condition.

Overlove is a mental illness that propels formerly sane men and women into the throes of insane jealousy, irrational behavior, bad health, drugs and alcohol, ruined credit, and time in jail.

Overlove has also bought many a poor soul a few shovels of dirt in Paupers' Field.

Overlove is an addiction—right on up there with drugs, alcohol, and food. Some people kill for overlove. Some die for it.

The aftereffects of overlove are the stuff of *People* magazine and *Hard Copy,* the tabloids and the talk shows.

It would seem that with all this attention, someone would surely have thought of a song about overlove by now.

I am frustrated with Brothers who fall into overlove with selfish FAAWABAs who will only gloat at their demise and hover over their carcasses like vultures.

[Wasting your life on such women is like tossing pennies to pigs in hopes that they'll use the money to clean the sty.]

I'm not telling you anything new; you know there are women who are so angry with men (for whatever reason) that they're sworn, like the legendary tribe of amazing Amazon women, to destroy them.

Men are meat. Men are currency. Men are the enemy.

[A FAAWABA definitely does not love her enemy.]

A Brother who falls for a FAAWABA is always trying to prove to her that he is enough for her. He is good enough, his car is nice enough, he has enough money, or he is brave enough to *deserve* her attention.

[For the overloving FAAWABA, "enough" is never enough. Her appetites can never be satisfied.]

Some of the devious methods these women use to ensnare

their men seem like lame excuses to the rest of us Sisters, but up until now, many Brothers have taken to these dangerous women like butter to a hot skillet.

When a man is falling into overlove, he ignores many of the early warning signs, even though there are issues in the relationship that seem to keep cropping up like weeds on a manicured lawn.

[He's taken her out once and called her twice, but she's turned into a beeper bomber, paging him every eight minutes.]

If you know a Blackman who is falling for any of these seven sad scenarios, Girlfriend, he is a candidate for the unfortunate club of rejection, rage, and pain that is the underworld of the overloved.

1. She couldn't help getting pregnant . . . again. She gets sick on the pill.
2. She is always getting fired because other women are jealous of her.
3. She can't stand criticism because her daddy always picked on her. Or she was Daddy's favorite.
4. You have to pick her up from work every day because she's afraid to drive in the big city.
5. She calls you at work fifty times a day because she has no one to talk to or because she is bored.
6. She overspends because she always used to have money, before her last divorce. Or before her mother died.
7. This amazingly healthy woman, who jogs five miles a day, is prone to migraine headaches only when you want to make love.

A woman who is versed in the craft of overlove often disguises herself as helpless, weak, and frail. She can't seem to do anything without a Brother's help.

[You big, strong daddy.]

Don't believe it!

This lady holds a third-degree black belt in overlove. She is delicately devious. She is ultra-rageously pious. At first she was as sweet as a packet of NutraSweet; now you recognize that she is, in fact, as sticky as flypaper.

[And you thought she was a virgin.]

She has mastered the art of manipulation and control through perfecting over one hundred different moods.

[Wait 'til you really get to know this Sistah, my man. You've only seen a fraction of the action.]

One male friend of mine finally left his wife of eight years when her obsessive behavior got so bad that she'd open his mail unapologetically and monitor his phone calls, breathing heavily on the extension if the caller was a woman.

In their decade together—as roommates, lovers, and spouses—my friend had lost many jobs because of his woman's erratic and jealous behavior.

He drop-kicked all of his buddies—including his fraternity brothers and siblings he'd grown up with—because his woman accused them of making advances on her.

[No man—not even his father—was above suspicion.]

Finally, he'd had enough.

[Remember "enough"?]

He planned a move for months, like a breakout from jail. While his overloving wife was at work, he packed his meager belongings and split—leaving her all the furniture, the CD collection, and every cooking utensil in the house.

But see, by this time their overlove was in overdrive, and it was the force driving him to distraction.

Over time, this Brother had made overlove the defense for his every failure, the excuse for each of his many miseries, and the reason for all of his shortcomings.

[Her overlove became his overexcuse.]

All in all, he missed the pain. After three months of bachelor calm and quiet, he tucked his ego between his legs and stumbled on home to his overlovin' wife.

Maybe if someone had written a song about overlove, this pitiful Brother might have ended up humming a happier tune.

I believe many of the casualties of overlove are preventable. Let me just warn my Sisters that there are signs that a Brother may be swapping his good sense for a bad trip.

As we cut to the chase, here are the most obvious overlove indicators. If you are involved with (or related to) a man who is involved in any of the following bizarre scenarios, please warn him that he is courting certain cataclysm. He is headed straight into the vise of overlove.

1. He can't help wondering where she is, who she's with, and what she's doing.
2. He is constantly trying to "prove" something to her, her family, and/or friends.
3. They fight more than they love, but it is obvious that he will go back for more.
4. She can always dish it out, and he will always take it.
5. He can't stand to be with her, but he can't stand her to be with anybody else.

Overlove may put a man in jail, but it'll spell suicide to a Sister.

[Maybe it's overlove that makes people call us the weaker sex.]

I want to warn Sisters about the disguises of overlove because overlove just may be the number-one killer of Blackwomen in the nineties.

I personally know dozens of my Sisters who've died of overlove (disguised as cancer, heart attacks, and strokes) brought on by terminal relationships with men.

Overlove in women parades around as abuse, assault, and battery.

[What do you mean, you won't testify against him?]

Electronically, overlove in women manifests itself as talk-show fodder.

["Homeboy beats Girlfriend and he is sleeping with her cousin, who is pregnant with his baby, but still she wants him back."]

Domestic violence plays so prominently in the news these days that I wonder why no one has stopped to make the connection between overphysical and overlove.

There has to be a point in all this madness when Sisters see that the easiest way to prevent abuse is to not become a victim.

Now, I'll admit that sometimes "victimization" is unavoidable. Like getting held up at an ATM machine at high noon, you just don't expect some crimes to happen, and you're never prepared.

But sometimes, just sometimes, Sisters do ask for trouble by wearing a flashing neon sign that spells out "V-i-c-t-i-m."

In fact, I've found that some reluctant abusers generously hold the door to freedom open for a fleeting moment, before putting a foot in your face.

He is begging not to do you harm. *"Don't make me hurt you now,"* he says. He is asking you to remove his temptation. *"If you know what's good for you, you'll get out of my face."*

[Girlfriend, are you really listening to what he's saying?]

All of the warning signs are on, your overloving man is sounding the alarm, and the gate is open—if only for a minute.

If a Sister has good sense, she will split in a lick before she becomes a statistic. But some victims will squat on the spot at the first signs of danger, preferring the security of bondage (to him) over the uncertainty of freedom alone.

Now I'm not belittling the tragic victims of domestic violence, and I'm certainly not condoning the acts of the perpetrator, but it seems to me that many intended victims (IVs) don't have to be cookie dough in an egg beater if they'll just heed the subtle early warning signs of abusive behavior.

Like a smoldering fire before it is ablaze or like a sheet of crusty water just before it turns to ice, there are usually obvious signs that your new main squeeze is looking at you like a ripened orange.

[You're thinking how sweet the romance is going to taste, and he's looking at you like pulp in the juice.]

I'll never forget the time I was stomped and sexually assaulted by a former boyfriend who must have been dyslexic. After a few months of pussyfooting around a breakup I finally said, "N-O more" and he heard "more O-N." And that's exactly what the Brother did.

It took me years to get over allowing myself to become rape bait for a man for whom I knew violence was a way of life.

[I'm not really blaming myself for my rape, but when Brother-Dog kicked the cat before we so much as left the flat for our first date, couldn't I see the next foot would be on me?]

Sisters who've fallen prey to overlove rarely admit that they saw it coming. But if you ask these pathetic IVs some history, they'll tell you that their abuser exhibited at least some of the early warning signs of bad days (and nights) to come.

[Check it out!]

TEN EARLY WARNING SIGNS OF OVERLOVE

1. He fell in love with you in thirty seconds. [Was it the color of your eyes or something you said?]
2. He calls you every hour. [You think he's being attentive, but he's really crazy.]
3. He makes frequent suggestions about your personal style or appearance. [Suggestions evolve into demands over time.]
4. He wants all of your time. [He needs to make love at least twice a day, and he hates your mama.]
5. He blames his past woman/women for not understanding or helping him to become successful. Or his ex-wife had a secret affair with the swing-shift manager at McDonald's. [Well, it's got to be someone's fault.]

6. He is moody, possessive, jealous, and too darned curious. [He sorts all your mail, screens your phone calls, takes detailed messages, and is always asking questions.]
7. He buys your affection and likes you to depend on him. [He'll buy you a cellular phone so he can keep track of you. He'll pay the mortgage on your own condo but put his name on the deed.]
8. He won't use sexual protection. [He doesn't carry any, and he refuses to discuss it.]
9. He wants you to be the mother of his baby. [He either grew up without a father and he can't wait to be a daddy, or he hasn't been allowed by his ex to spend any time with his other kids.]
10. You find a $500,000 double-indemnity life insurance policy drawn on your life, naming him as the sole beneficiary, tucked away in his sock drawer.

If you feel yourself slipping into the septic tank of overlove, there *is* something you can do to pull yourself back from the sewer.

If you are being racked and ravaged by overlove, you first have to admit that you are no good to anyone, least of all yourself, while you are so afflicted. Unless you get help, you will be permanently disabled.

You only *think* that you are functioning as a normal person.

[Those migraine headaches, nervous twitches, hemorrhoids, ulcers, and the three bottles of Mylanta stashed in your drawer should tell you that something ain't right.]

If you can be objective for a minute, you can clearly see that under the whip of the overlover, you are the walking wounded or the living dead.

You don't deserve to live in such tortured madness.

[Remember what it was like to wake up to birds singing instead of to screaming, crying, and a clenched fist?]

How would it feel to know that no one had been rummaging

through your personal things? Or how about having a little nest egg in the bank for something other than a disaster?

Life without overlove is a far cry from nirvana, to be sure, but it beats life in the spin cycle any day of the week.

The point is, you can recover from an addiction to overlove. Hundreds of thousands of people have turned their lives around, finding meaningful, satisfying, and peaceful relationships that fulfill their every fantasy and don't cause chronic indigestion. Why, they don't even miss the chaos.

Now, I'm not suggesting that my recovery plan is the only way to combat the ravages of overlove, but it has only three simple steps, so what do you have to lose?

THE THREE-STEP OVERLOVE RECOVERY PROGRAM

1. Don't make any rash or hasty decisions. Don't move, get married or divorced, spend an enormous amount of money on anything, kill anyone, or buy a gun. Don't even hire a private detective. [If you *think* your lover is cheating, chances are you're right, and you haven't spent a dime.]
2. Stay busy and fit. Exercise and nourish your body, mind, and spirit with wholesome activities that are life-giving and love-enforcing.
3. Punish your overlover with your success. Make a vow to deliver a wallop of the unexpected right into the face of the lover who told you that you'd never be anything without her or him. In the final analysis, your happiness is the best revenge.

---

16 CONDOMPHOBIA AND INTIMACY IN THE AIDS GENERATION

As we grow older, that old biological clock ticking down the years often makes us cling to the next man who smiles and speaks English.

Don't let the Brother have a job and be single!

The Sisters jump the Brother like a hawk on a wounded chicken.

Jumping on him, my Sister, or letting him jump on you is, these days, as dangerous as playing footsie with a rattlesnake in your sleeping bag.

This is the AIDS generation—not the sixties, when it was cool to go from the streets to the sheets in one easy night.

There's just nothing easy about sex these days. The threat of AIDS has taken the fun out of fun 'n' games.

In the nineties you can't afford to trip on sex like a summer vacation.

[A romp or two and then you're through.]

Nowadays every season of promiscuity carries a possible death sentence.

Not enough people, outside of the talk-show circuit, are talking about sex these days. Not even in the bedroom. Most folks aren't talking; they are just doing *It*.

Still doing It! And quite frankly, I don't get it.

I mean, this is the AIDS generation, Girlfriend, and we've been pounded with enough warning information by the entire medical community and the media for all of us to be well informed.

It is obvious to me that in the AIDS generation, people are not getting the message.

Some Brothers are in strong denial about AIDS or any other incurable disease. To these sexual gladiators, life is still a continual sexual feast, even after the "Magic revelation" of 1991. Even after Easy-E in 1995.

Sadly, many of these warriors of wanderlust are Brothers of means. In fact, it is their money that gives them the means to enjoy the fruits of their affluence to the fullest.

Sex, for these gents, is a status symbol—right along with membership in the country club, the Mercedes Benz, Bali shoes, and the American Express Gold Card.

[Some wolf-whiffing Brothers change women like most people change socks.]

I'm not talking just single satyrs either, my Sisters. I'm talking married (with children) men and men in (otherwise) committed relationships.

It seems that most guys don't believe AIDS can catch them with their pants down.

And they are not alone. Many Sisters are going to get caught with their skirts up, too.

Some Sisters, I've noticed, are afraid not to do *It*. There are so many Sisters who will do *It* and so few Brothers who don't demand *It* that some Blackwomen feel they have to give it up to get asked to dance.

To these Sisters my question is this: If you are *giving* it away, what makes you think he owes you anything?

[Free is free. Right?]

Other Sisters do *It* to pay the rent or the car note. Or to eat in a gourmet restaurant; to get invited to an exclusive party; to ride in a fine car. They're not hooking, really. They've just got a financial agenda. And the sex is nothing more than currency.

In a growing number of cases, Sisters are afraid of the reduction of lifestyle after a divorce. They don't want to lose the car, give up the house, or take the kid out of private school.

To lose a man is one thing; to lose a credit card is quite another. So they buy time by selling their bodies—and selling their lives.

Still walking amidst us are those slutty Sisters who will give it up faster than a compulsive shopper in a ninety-nine-cent store.

And don't let me forget the weekend players who are celibate for whole five-day stretches at a time. They are addicted to love and are drawn to sex like syrup to a pancake. They soak it up and never get enough.

It is amazing to me how many excuses folks use to trivialize sex, without exercising the slightest bit of caution.

It seems to me that we're more cautious about how we eat than with whom we sleep.

[You wouldn't eat with someone else's fork, would you?]

I'm no prude, but abstinence to me makes good health sense in the nineties. But for those who are going to do *It,* do *It* right.

[Girl, if you could only see me beggin'.]

For his sake and for your sake, carry a condom as close as your comb and your lipstick. And use it with the same regularity.

[And just think, nobody ever died from not wearing lipstick.]

Condoms are as essential to lovemaking in the nineties as birth control pills were in the sixties.

Please don't leave home without them.

Sadly, buying a condom and using it are two separate issues today. According to most surveys, while most singles talk condoms and safe sex, neither men nor women actually use protection.

Men in heat don't think about condoms as a part of their wardrobe. And women who do carry condoms are often too embarrassed to use them.

[Even in the nineties, it's Monkey Business as usual.]

With AIDS on the rise in the heterosexual Black community, I am led to the conclusion that we suffer from a new disease: *condomphobia*—the fear of condoms.

Far too many Brothers and Sisters are scared to use condoms.

Some simply play Russian roulette with their lives. But most people just don't seem to think about the lethal ramifications of their sexual actions.

Do you realize that most people—men and women—lie more about their sexual history to prospective partners than they do about their income to the IRS?

[Told any recent fish stories yourself, Girlfriend?]

Say he's married—and screwing around with you! Are you the only Sister he's fooling around with? And do you insist that he use a condom *every* time you make love?

OK, now say you're the wife of a man who is fooling around. [Are you fooling around too, by the way?]

Oh, yes, and do you *always* insist on condom use with your spouse? With your lover?

Sadly, far too many Brothers and Sisters suffering from condomphobia are still in denial about the AIDS epidemic. They are clearly out of touch with the AIDS generation. And today, being out of touch is a terminal mistake.

AIDS, as a growing number of heterosexuals can testify, is a family disease and an equal-opportunity killer.

Girlfriend, Girlfriend, if you want to pamper your Blackman, protect him and yourself from the ultimate death sentence. Be the first Sister in your circle of friends to insist on protection.

Your man may protest. He may object. The Brother may tell you that he hasn't had sex in six years—since he left the monastery. He *knows* he's safe. He wonders about you. He's hurt that you don't trust him.

He may show you his most recent health certificate and swear on his mother's life that he wouldn't hurt you.

The jury is out on *how* you instantly change your long-held sexual practices. And getting your macho man to accept a rubber raincoat—even though he thinks the sun is shining between the sheets—is not without risk. But risk you must.

[Risk the relationship, or perish from the plague.]

I've asked hundreds of Sisters how they handle this delicate issue. Most are rather cut-and-dried. (No pun intended.)

"No protection, no affection," say some realistic Sisters.

"No glove, no love," say others.

Only one Sister, in fact, so moved me that I want to share her experience.

This Sister admitted that she had been phobic about condoms until a few years ago—when she discovered her former lover leaving a gay bar.

"That did it," she declared. "I thought the guy was as straight as a ruler. If I could be wrong about him, I could be wrong about anyone."

This conscious woman conquered her phobia overnight. Today she wouldn't be caught dead in bed without a condom.

I asked her how she approached the subject with lovers and other would-be intimate partners.

"When the conversation rolls around to sex," she says, "I tell my companion *that* story. And I always tell him that it only happened just three months ago.

"I look at him sweetly and say, 'Baby, I don't want you to be at risk.'"

Some Brothers, she says, don't mind taking the risk.

"If they'd take a risk on me," she says, "they're definitely too risky for me."

Some Brothers, she says, run an Olympic mile to get away from her. Those men, she figures, aren't worth playing with anyway.

Like the marines, she figures, she only needs a few good men.

Those are the ones who appreciate her "confession" and will certainly take precautions. These Brothers, she says, even thank her for her honesty, and a few come clean themselves.

From a possible tragedy, this Sister has constructed a litmus test for intimacy.

Now, I'm sure that there are more subtle (and less devious) ways of enticing your gentleman to use protection.

You might tell him that you've just taken a megadose of fertility pills and unless he wants to be the daddy of sextuplets, you advise him to use a condom.

You might bone up on the latest AIDS statistics and have a few policy papers conveniently placed on the nightstand.

Or you might even tell him the truth—that you have no plans to become an AIDS statistic.

The point is, now, as a full-fledged member of the AIDS generation, you can't afford to get cold feet or be weak in the knees on this issue. You've got to take a real stand to conquer condomphobia.

I've found that the easiest way of overcoming any phobia is to reach out and grab hold of the situation.

If your Brother won't voluntarily change his sexual dressing habits, my hands-on advice on how to cure him of condomphobia is to get a grip on that bad boy and take matters into your own hands. The control, dear Sister, is at your fingertips.

Because *Himpressions: The Blackwoman's Guide to Pampering the Blackman* is truly a user's manual, I am duty bound to share with my Sisters fifty ways of overcoming even the most ardent proposal of *sack-jacking*.

Hijacking, skyjacking, and carjacking are all a part of high-risk life in the nineties, right? Well, then, *sack-jacking* is sexual terrorism that deserves the same publicity and condemnation as these other heinous crimes.

FIFTY WAYS TO SAY NO TO SEX

1. No.
2. I discovered that my last lover was bisexual.
3. My heart and I have this understanding.
4. I'm not old enough.
5. I suffer from cold feet.
6. I'm climbing Mount Rushmore in the morning.
7. My father is the West Coast director of the NRA.
8. My last six kids were conceived using contraception.
9. No one can satisfy me like I can.
10. Jocelyn Elders is my shero.
11. Masturbation is my greatest form of entertainment.
12. Sex makes me itch.
13. Sex makes me throw up within thirty seconds of the act.
14. I'm a vegetarian.
15. I don't think I'd love you in the morning.
16. I don't think you'd love me after midnight.
17. My life is complicated enough as it is.
18. I have an appointment to get my hair done.
19. My baby brother is the leader of the Crips.
20. What was your name again?
21. Chocolate and semen don't mix.
22. Nice girls don't.
23. I'm practicing to become a nun.
24. I've got a virgin complex.
25. My kids would kill me.
26. I gain too much weight.
27. I'm allergic to sweat.
28. I'm allergic to sugar.
29. I don't want to ruin our friendship.
30. I don't have time to do a follow-up call.
31. I can't make love and breathe at the same time.
32. After I see current health certificates of the last three hundred women you've slept with.
33. Have you seen *The Crying Game*?

34. Watch how I can pamper you with your pants on.
35. My lips are sealed.
36. I'm afraid you'd get me so hot that I might incinerate.
37. I might not remember that I liked you.
38. I want to live to see the year 2000.
39. I can't afford the mortgage and a hospital bill.
40. I hate to eat and run.
41. I hate to eat on the run.
42. I pray over all of my sex partners first.
43. I'd just fall asleep.
44. It's never as much fun as it looks in the movies.
45. My pit bull is sensitive to loud noises.
46. I get nose bleeds.
47. I'm happier healthy.
48. I always call my mother first.
49. This is the second day of my ten-year moratorium on sex.
50. No, no, no, no, no. What part of n-o don't you understand?

17 GOOD-BYE . . . GOOD-BYE . . . GOOD-BYE AGAIN: WHEN IT'S TIME TO LEAVE

I don't care how great it was between you, when it's over it's over. Learn to love generously and leave graciously.

I once had an otherwise intelligent friend who loved a certain Brother more than a baby loves milk. The problem was, the feeling wasn't mutual.

The Sister nagged her way into a wedding band, but almost before the honeymoon sheets were changed, the Brother was asking for a divorce.

During one final moment of passion, she poked a hole in her diaphragm. Lo and behold the Sister became pregnant.

Quietly accepting his fate, the Brother stopped asking for a divorce. As a matter of fact, he stopped everything—arguing, eating at home, talking to her. He stayed away for days, then weeks, at a time.

Less than a year after their daughter's birth, it came as no surprise to anyone when he announced that he was moving out.

My now-emotional-wreck-of-a-friend took a disability leave from her job, entered therapy, but still spent her days and nights plotting against her ex and his slender new girlfriend.

Her disposition was so disagreeable that the Brother took to visiting his daughter at the home of his former mother-in-law, at first on request and then on demand of the court.

Now Sister-Girl really went crazy. First she got fired. Then she had a nervous breakdown.

In and out of mental institutions for the past twelve years, this once-attractive Sister now looks thirty years older than she really is, and no one wants her except her pharmacist.

Today, the Brother and his pretty young wife have custody of his child. They live in a beautiful house in suburban Los Angeles, with his firstborn daughter and a son of their own.

Life goes on!

Another friend spent years plotting how to get her man back into her arms. She could not accept his claim that he no longer loved her.

Eight years later, on his wedding day to a woman he'd known for less than a month, he still didn't love my friend.

Just imagine the positive, self-enhancing things she could have done with those eight years.

She could have gone through medical school with all the energy she'd invested into getting her ex-boyfriend back into her arms.

[I think of a failed love affair as a meal. Yesterday's lunch is today's bowel movement. That doesn't mean that it wasn't good; it's just over. Flush!]

The best you can do, my Sisters, is maintain your dignity when it's time to part. Let him remember you as a lady.

Having been in this position too many times to count, I can tell you, groveling makes you hate yourself and him too—you for doing it; him for witnessing it.

Besides, who are you mad at anyway? Him for leaving? Or yourself for ignoring the signs?

Think about it.

There were signs, of course. There are always signs.

Where once he hung on your every word, he now hangs you by your words.

Remember when he called you five times a day? Now you call him once and he's busy.

At the height of your romance, he always bought tickets for two. Now he needs his space.

Now the only flowers, love notes, and wine labels you have are the ones pressed into your book of memories.

He is bored. He is glum. He is passive. He is sad. Angry. Irritable. Distracted. He is gaining weight, or he's losing his temper. He's absentminded, he's late, or he's gone.

Girlfriend, if your Blackman is tired, maybe he's just tired of you!

I don't need to tell you, dear Sister, you may not know where he is coming from, but you know that he's going.

And you may not know where he's going, but you know that his heart is already out the door.

So what are you going to do about it? You've lost your grip as you watch the luster of love slip into a state of rust.

Some sad Sisters opt for revenge. Revenge, they say, is sweet.

But the thrill of getting even lasts no longer than the thrill of taking a plunge off a fifty-foot cliff. It is a cheap thrill that causes a lot of damage.

Causing him misery or getting even is certain emotional suicide for you too. If he didn't care for you before, your reviling acts of terrorism, subterfuge, and sabotage will only brand you as a malcontent or lunatic.

[Please see chapter 15, "Overlove."]

This is a tough one, my Sisters. And many of you will argue that I've missed the mark. You feel you have to make him pay for the shabby way he treated you.

But let's look at the short and the long terms of your cheap thrill.

What's the Brother going to think about you when the door slams shut? And what will you think of yourself, say, in ten years or so, when you bump into him on the street? Or you are reintroduced at a party?

A certain Sister I know planned revenge on her former boyfriend down to the microscopic detail. She kept a list of revolting acts in a little journal she liked to show her friends.

I remember only a few of her pranks: sugar in his gas tank, rotten eggs thrown against his house, telegrams charged to his telephone number, and a number of midnight calls to disturb his sleep.

Twenty years later, I was told, she had to face that same Brother over a desk. Unwittingly she had applied for a job for which she was imminently qualified. Her former boyfriend was the newly hired vice president of personnel.

[Life certainly offers interesting little twists, doesn't it?]

In this case, the Sister wove her own noose and then hung herself with it twenty years later.

Now, finally, after a hundred or so relationships—of greater or lesser degrees of intimacy—I've finally learned that *good-bye* is a beautiful word.

If only we could take *good-bye,* like art, at face value, instead of trying to rework it to fit our egos.

Sisters today don't understand the lengths a Brother will go to get away, if he wants to leave. He will run, hide, move, change his name, anything to make tracks away from a Sister he no longer wants to be bothered with.

You can pout. You can stomp. You can cry or faint. You can threaten. You can beg. You can burn his clothes or call South Africa from his telephone. When the Brother wants to get his hat, that's that.

Just ask any Brother. There are more than fifty ways to leave your lover.

So, if there is nothing you can do to get him back, why not just let him go?

The least you can do—with words or in silence—is maintain your dignity. Don't get caught up in the emotions of the moment.

Sometimes you just can't keep quiet. You've got to speak the words. Even if he has cotton mouth, you have a few silky words to share in the final moments of your affair.

Now if you can't seem to get the words out—because there's too much pain or too much emotion behind them—how about writing a loving letter?

[You'll feel liberated just writing it. You don't even have to mail it.]

It's your play, but don't let that be your excuse for bad behavior. Your last great act of pampering the Brother should be to leave your positive prints on his memory.

[OK, so you flubbed that last one. You don't have to repeat all your errors, do you?]

I know several Sisters who maintain close friendly relationships with a number of their ex-boyfriends.

[And I'm proud to say that I'm one of 'em.]

They can ask a favor, get an escort, or make a new business buddy out of their former lovers with ease.

The door, for these smart Sisters, is always open because they didn't break the man's arm off when it was closing.

They have the uncanny ability to turn sour grapes into sweet grape juice.

For them the simple philosophy is this: you can only grow from hearing "no." These ladies would rather ponder joy than dwell in misery.

[They won't be done in by a breakup.]

I watched one Sister go through such a difficult parting with a man who said he no longer cared for her. She had assumed their three-month-old relationship had a future. She was committed.

But he was committed only to play the field after he hit a home run.

I watched her go through several emotional stages: she was dismayed—stunned—shocked. Then she was so hurt that she became angry at herself for her naïveté. In one week, however, she waxed philosophical.

"You know, since he doesn't like me," she said one day, "it was really kind of him to let me get on with my life."

And that's exactly what she did, with a smile.

The Brother was so shocked by her reaction he couldn't leave her alone. They became the best of friends. Finally this good Brother came to his senses and realized that he had the pick of the pack. Today they are, by most accounts, successfully married, expecting their second child.

Of course, most romances don't have such tight storybook endings.

I have another friend who has this philosophy, which she shares with each new love interest: "I may be easy to leave, but I'm hard to forget."

This lady confesses that most of the men she's been close to can't get used to being treated well. (See chapter 11, "WAAWABAs in Your Midst.") She admits that almost every Brother she's been with has left her for a cute, clinging, nagging, and possessive little shrew in sheep's clothing. (See chapter 10, "Beware the FAAWABA!")

As the romance wears thin, she says, she simply steps aside.

The amazing thing is that in time, they all come back. Only then do they remember her words. See, when she turns the page (on a relationship), she also closes the book.

This Sister is proud to say that she is on friendly terms with all of her former boyfriends.

Now, I'll admit, my Sister, that men don't necessarily play by our rules. Maybe he dogged you. Maybe he stole your money. Maybe he forgot to mention that he's married.

[Oops!]

The point is, you did get something out of it, didn't you?

[In every little loss there is a bigger lesson.]

In the nineties' era of fierce competition, you've got to throw out that old rule book. Today the play is either to wallow in self-pity or to dust off your ego and get back out on the field. Those, dear Sister, are often the only two choices you have.

Life goes on. It really does.

If you really want to get the knack of pampering the Blackman, learn to recognize a once-sweet song turning into a broken record.

When the music stops, there is only one sensible thing to do. Don't forget the tune, but turn off the radio and preserve your batteries.

The fact is, Girlfriend, that we are all living in the fast lane. In any relationship, you don't have to go the distance together in order to enjoy the ride.

18 WHATEVER HAPPENED TO PUPPY LOVE?

I was becoming afraid that puppy love had gone the way of carbon typing paper, black-and-white television, and Blue Chip stamps. They all seem to be extinct in the nineties.

[I tried to sell a full box of carbon paper at my last garage sale, but I couldn't even *give* the stuff away!]

Unlike carbon paper, black-and-white TVs, and Blue Chip stamps, however, I see a definite place for puppy love in the nineties.

See, puppy love, in today's era of hypersex and galvanized love, is a way of putting the brakes on a relationship that is moving too darned fast.

[How are you gonna pamper yourself or anyone while you're rollin' down a ravine at one hundred miles an hour?]

If you look at too many talk shows or public trials, if you read only the bad news and listen to too many miserable people, you'll take the cynical low road and look at the obvious: puppy love in the nineties has given way to doggie lust.

[Today, it seems that everyone is just doin' *It* in the ravine at one hundred miles an hour.]

★   ★   ★

I'll admit that I miss the good old days (the sixties) when a girl could be coquettish and play charming little mind games before she allowed anything physical to transpire—like holding hands.

Riding home from church with a boy, listening to early Motown and Philadelphia sounds on the car radio, our greatest fear was that we would get our white gloves dirty. Now that was pure puppy love!

Puppy love was playing footsie in a darkened theater. It was midnight telephone conversations, voluminous letters, giggling, and ultralong walks together, where birds sang opera and time evaporated.

Puppy love was walking into *like* before you fell into *love*.

If passion is a grease-soaked salad, puppy love was love lite.

Perhaps the greatest thing about puppy love was that the person didn't really have to puppy-love you back. He didn't even have to know that you had a crush on him. Like falling for a movie star or a campus basketball hero, your infatuation was strictly between you and your girlfriends.

Puppy lovin' for every generation up to and including the baby boomers was one of those precourtship rituals that could stretch the first kiss out for six months.

Like an old, classic Spencer Tracy–Katharine Hepburn movie, puppy love was fun, it was wholesome. It was romantic. It was innocent.

[And nobody ever got pregnant from puppy love.]

To tell you the truth, Girlfriend, some folks think of puppy love as an immature infatuation, but in the nineties, developing a case of puppy love before you develop a case of doggie lust may be one of those antiquated precourtship rituals that could stand some dusting off.

Now I'm no puppy-lovin' expert, although we baby boomers did have some pretty good role models, and I was a good student. Femme fatales such as Dorothy Dandridge, Marilyn Monroe, and Diana Ross and the Supremes led a generation of girls into womanhood and perfection in the subtle art of the demure downward glance, the coy eyelash flicker, and the pert pout.

[In days of old, these quiet poses were wordless demonstrations of a lady's interest in a member of the opposite sex.]

During the sixties, one of my college roommates kept herself in Estée Lauder perfume by customizing a puppy-love curriculum for her dorm sisters. Girlfriend guaranteed that at the end of twelve weeks (half a semester), you'd have your pooch eating out of your hand.

Like any time-tested theory that becomes an axiom for all ages, many of Pamela's Puppy-Love Control Program tips still work.

PAMELA'S TWELVE-WEEK PUPPY-LOVE CONTROL PROGRAM

Week 1: You pretend that he doesn't exist.

Week 2: You coyly acknowledge that he does exist, and you smile.

Week 3: Once you know that he's interested, you say "hello" but don't stop to make conversation.

Week 4: You act totally surprised when you find out that he's the secret admirer who sent you flowers.

Week 5: You talk briefly on the phone but have to dash.

Week 6: You flirt with him when you meet for coffee.

Week 7: You talk on the phone for three hours in one of the silliest conversations you've ever had with a man.

Week 8: You meet for lunch.

Week 9: Your first date is something physical—like roller skating, playing tennis, or dancing.

Week 10: You cook for him on Saturday night and hold hands while watching television.

Week 11: He cooks for you the following Sunday.

Week 12: Your puppy is ready for his leash.

Some people would argue with me that puppy love has gone the way of the one-penny parking meter and ten-cent phone call, but I optimistically believe that its revival just may be at hand.

See, in the nineties, puppy love may be the only kind of relationship with the opposite sex that doesn't have any lasting negative ramifications.

Think about it, Girlfriend. Puppy love is a way to really get to know someone, letting the relationship simmer and steep before pouring it into your love cup.

Puppy love may also be the best way for a Sister to rid herself of a potential serial moocher or a wolf-whiffer disguised as a nice guy. [A hungry dog will not wait to eat.]

After interviewing dozens of couples who admitted that their relationships started as puppy love, and they're all still holding hands, I've been looking for a way to peddle puppy love to today's hip young Sisters.

But to tell the truth, I'd all but given up on developing a nineties model of behavior for this admittedly old-fashioned custom that would sit well with today's modern Ms.

For the two or three generations of Sisters who don't have any recollection of love without sex, my proposition to slow down the chase to a snail's saunter is laughable.

[Some young Sisters today don't want to listen to an old puppy lover like me. They are being schooled in doggie lust by a cadre of TV talk-show guests—roto-heads and hoochie mamas with X-rated body language.]

Just as I was lamenting the passage of the Age of Puppy Love, I had a catch-up conversation with one of my Generation-X girlfriends that rekindled my fire.

Was I dreaming? Had my prayers been answered? Puppy love, in the nineties, in renaissance!?

[It was true! There was a filling at the root of the cavity.]

After two years of avoiding intimate contact with the opposite sex—because of sweet relationships gone sour—my retro-virgin X-er girlfriend was finally getting personal with a Brother.

She told me that although most of her friends thought she was out there with Dr. Spock, she was developing a long-term, long-distance case of puppy love over the Internet.

"It started innocently enough," she explained. "I was just hanging out in one of the on-line board rooms for a couple of weeks, checking out the cyberfreaks, when *he* asked to meet me privately."

"We've been logged in for nearly six months," she said.

"Well, do you like him?" I asked.

She was evasive. Coy. Just like I used to be when I was playing puppy-love games in the sixties.

"I'm not getting a cyberfix or anything like that," she said, "but he's a really interesting Brother."

"Aren't you bored," I asked, "just talking?"

Her private giggle reminded me of my first experience with puppy love. [I stretched that one out for two years and never did get naked.]

"Oh, we do more than just chat," she gushed.

Although Homeboy lives in Ohio and Girlfriend in L.A., the happy couple have been doing a lot of on-line longing in their reclusive little room.

"I'm extremely impressed," she giggled, "with his proclivity for virtual reality."

She won't tell me everything, although I'm plenty curious. But she did say that after a couple of months of small talk, they are doing a lot of cybersmooching these days.

[Does cybersmooching, I wonder, lead, like in the old days, to cyberlove? Or to cybersex?]

Get with the program, I tell myself. So long as the results of a cyberrelationship is not a baby cyborg, I've got to go along with the X-ers on their new spin of our old tune.

Thanks to a new generation of Brothers and Sisters who appreciate the pleasures of pampering each other via E-mail, I am now pleasantly convinced that puppy love is alive and well and living in a computer chip.

AFTERWORD

In conclusion . . .

Now, you know that's a lie. *Himpressions: The Blackwoman's Guide to Pampering the Blackman* is only the first installment of my thoughts on Black relationships—as a Blackwoman, writer, wife, and mother of a man-child.

The truth is, I'm just getting warmed up.

Like talking on the phone to a friend you haven't spoken to in five years, you want to stay up all night playing "catch-up."

Credentialwise, I'm just another Blackwoman. Although my training and background in communications qualifies me to comment on relationships from a social science point of view, my propositions are based on sense, not science. It is the sense we all have but too infrequently use. Common sense has become, all too often, quite uncommon.

Certainly we all have a lot to say about the troubled state of Black male-female relationships. It is my great hope that this guide inspires people to say what's on their minds. I believe that the time for silence is past.

It doesn't much matter if you approve or disapprove, like or dislike this writer's *himpressions.* I hope, in fact, that you'll pick my ideas apart like a piece of meat stuck between your teeth.

I'll be a happy camper if you just think about them. And if anything I have to say works for another Sister or helps a relationship to survive in these chaotic times, then my *himpressions* have been worth sharing.

In keeping with the brevity of this manual and in hopes that a Sister can glean just one idea that will enhance her relationship with a Brother, I've condensed the essence of my *himpressions* into a pocket-size list of twenty do's and don'ts. I call them "Himpression Nuggets."

Although they've all been said a thousand times before in a thousand different ways—like "I love you" in a song—you can listen and listen but you can't hear it enough.

The truth is, you could possibly condense this entire book into a three-panel cartoon, a song, or a painting. I suppose it could take any form. But I'm a writer, not a cartoonist, songwriter, or artist.

So, in case you are the type of Sister who turns straight to the back of the book, I'll cut to the chase.

[Lord knows, I don't want any of my girlfriends to have an excuse not to read some part of this manual.]

So, Sister-Girl, if quick is it for you, I invite you to spend thirty seconds digesting a few morsels of "Himpression Nuggets."

And we've put in a little glossary for all you literary Sisters who are word freaks. Or maybe you just want to refresh your memory. I certainly don't want any of my Sisters to forget what a *wolf-whiffer* is, in case you should run into him.

[As you no doubt will, perhaps before the day is over.]

Then, if you still haven't had enough of my silliness, try your turn at the delightful "Workbook Exercises" or one of the several questionnaires sprinkled throughout the manual.

[Did you say you have nothing to talk about at the party, Girlfriend? Try one of these games!]

But please don't take our exercises in pampering too seriously—although I do hope you'll have some serious fun.

If you've been paying any attention, nothing in this *Guide to*

Pampering is too serious. Nothing, that is, except its intent.

It is with the most solemn of intents that I have presented my *himpressions*. And every word I've written is, in fact, a prayer. If any one of them can make a difference in any Sister's life, my heart will swell with pride.

D o . . .

1. be inventive, clever, and creative. Do the thoughtful things that require your imagination.
2. bend like a tree in matters of preference. But be hard as a rock in matters of principle.
3. smile. Laugh. Remember, sunshine can even melt snow.
4. be yourself—inside and out. Get clean and natural. Save the thirty dollars you were going to spend on acrylic fingernails for a dinner out or a gift of love.
5. clean up your act; clean up your flat. He may live like a pig, but your home should be a refuge from his sty.
6. cherish every moment of your time together. Become a time ecologist—don't waste it arguing, harboring jealousy, or trying to manipulate the moment.
7. want the best for him. If you are the best, what a team you'll make! If you're not, find a new field to play in.
8. unless you have happy, secure, and caring friends or family, leave your business at home. Remember, misery loves to meddle.

9. help! The Blackman needs help in the nineties as never before. We all do. Discarded, damaged, and skeptical, we are waging war on economic, psychological, and spiritual fronts. You can assist in the healing by helping. [Just ask any *one* of the participants in the historic Million Man March.]

10. hold the relationship in the same esteem you hold your job. The same etiquette applies: show up on time, do your share of the work, and make a positive contribution to the team.

D ON'T . . .

1. take the *stuff* so seriously. Be serious about one thing: being happy. In the Bible, this is reinforced in Proverbs 15:15: "A merry heart hath a continual feast." There will always be *stuff* and a lot of it—like sickness, loss of a job, the weather. Some things you just can't control. Learn to roll with the waves of change, and you'll be a survivor on the sea of life.

2. carry old baggage into your new hotel suite. His-story, her-story—it's all history.

3. be selfish. Now, "self first" is not being selfish, but if you insist on being Queen of the Me's, be prepared to reign over an empty court.

4. count on perfection. Lord knows, you're not perfect. Remember, everything in nature is flawed, including nature's grandest masterpieces. To the cynical, the Grand Canyon is just a bunch of jagged rocks. Imperfection is another word for individuality.

5. judge the horse by its saddle. Many wonderful catches drive a bus, deliver mail, or dig ditches. Take a few turns around the corral, and you may be surprised to learn that the quiet, Toyota-driving cowboy over there belongs to a

credit union, has great health benefits, and quite often has a little hustle on the side. He may do landscaping on the weekends, real estate during off hours, or tax preparation during the season.

6. nag. Oh, yeah, add "whine" to this one. Especially at inappropriate times. For one thing, a whining, nagging woman is sure to be ignored. Men hate it. By the way, never, never call him on the job with a complaint. It may be your dime, but what can he do on the boss's time?

7. let sex sink your relationship. You may be good, Sister, but to hold a man's attention these days, you better have more rap than just in the bedroom.

8. place your blooming fresh romance in a hothouse. Savor every step of its unfolding. It may be twice as nice if you put it on ice.

9. expect to get your size-eight feet into a size-six shoe. If the shoes don't fit, get yourself another pair that does. Not every relationship is 'til death do you part.

10. lose your upper hand by taking your fortune for granted. If you are blessed with a man who loves and respects you, you are holding an ace. When you treat him like a king, you are his queen. With the three most powerful trump cards in the deck, the only way you can lose is to throw away your hand. [Don't be a joker.]

Words, it seems to me, are the way we define our world. When words fail us, it leads to frustration, ulcers, and, increasingly, to blind rage.

Just watch a child trying to get a point across to an adult. A tantrum results when the kid tries and tries to make the grown-up get it and he just can't seem to explain himself.

[And how about all those fired, fired-up sickos who return to work at the post office with a twelve-gauge shotgun?]

Without the ability to communicate, in the absence of words, we have enormous difficulty describing how we feel. Words, it seems to me, are the gateway to our feelings. Once we have put our feelings into words, we can deal appropriately with our emotional response.

I mean, if you can't talk about a problem, how are you going to solve it?

[And how are you going to step into a healthy relationship when you're still draggin' your feet in the last sick one?]

It wasn't until I wrote the first edition of *Himpressions: The Blackwoman's Guide to Pampering the Blackman* that I began to realize how out of touch lexicographers are with the evolution of Black folks' interpersonal relationships.

These guys fully admit that advances in science and technology, sociological and political upheavals have had vast lexical consequences. So even the lexicographers concede that they're not the last word on words.

[Personally, I wonder how many lexicographers are Black.]

Even updated dictionaries don't help us define the predicament we're in these days. What with epidemic teenage pregnancy, runaway crime, poverty, and homelessness, not to mention a plethora of plagues raging over the planet, we'd do well to consider bringing in a fresh team of lexicographers.

In a partial move to make their lives easier—and, selfishly, to get my input out there early, before the committee meets—*Himpressions* has introduced many mutant words and terms and reintroduced several fine old-fashioned words that have fallen out of vogue, in the hope that you, the reader, will deem them worthy of use.

And besides, what's a *manual* without a *glossary*?

Beemer. A BMW.

Benz-o. A Mercedes Benz.

bust a move. Get busy.

condomphobia. Fear of using sexual protection.

cordial. Congenial; warm; friendly. (See *nice.*)

coquette. A flirt; tease.

courtship. The act of dating with the intent to become more serious over time.

coy. Bashful; modest. (See *demure.*)

cyberfix. The rush or high obtained by a computer junkie who turns on to the Internet.

cyberfreak. A computer junkie whose primary relationships take place on the privacy of a computer screen.

cyberlove. A deep affection developed by two people communicating strictly through the Internet.

cybersex. An ultra-personal computer-generated relationship, usually X-rated.

cybersmooch. Kissing on the Internet.

demure. Bashful; modest; reserved. (See *coy.*)

diss. To disrespect, dismiss, or disregard.

dissperception. A disparaging judgment made about someone based on false information.

dog. A wild man who disrespects women. (See *wolf-whiffer.*)

dogcatcher. A woman who is only attracted to dogs.

dumpee. A person who has been dumped.

FAAWABA. Acronym for Ferocious African-American Woman with a Bad Attitude; a wild woman who disrespects everyone.

FAAWABAdectomy. Personality reconstruction.

failureholic. One who is addicted to failure.

galvanized love. Lust.

incidental target. A nice guy (or gal) who attempts to stand between a Sister (or Brother) and a dog (or a FAAWABA).

IV. Intended victim.

himpressions. The feelings, views, and perceptions of Blackwomen regarding Blackmen.

hoochie mama. A FAAWABA who can't be sexually restrained.

hypersex. Crazy love; an unusually strong sexual appetite.

love lite. Puppy love, infatuation.

Loving Void. The necessary bridge between a discarded relationship and the future.

maledom. A dominion dominated by men.

NSA. Not sexually active. (See *retro-virgin.*)

negatron. Negative electron (energy).

nice. Congenial; friendly; dependable; an old-fashioned term for a person who respects others.

O.G. Original gangster.

outsight. The way one views the world; opposite of *insight.*

overlove. Obsessive and irrational longing for another. (See *sprung.*)

pamper. To nurture; to consider; to be thoughtful of.

pampership. The state of pampering.

propers. An old-fashioned word for *respect.*

puppy love. A mild infatuation; a crush. (See *love lite.*)

raincoat. Condom.

retro-virgin. A person who has recommitted himself or herself to celibacy; not an actual virgin. (See *NSA.*)

road-gal. A homegirl; running buddy.

roto-head. The nodding, bobbing, and other cranial contortions of a FAAWABA, common on tasteless TV talk shows.

sack-jacker. A sexual terrorist; a person who intimidates or cajoles another into committing a sexual act.

serial moocher. A chronic abuser of others' time, money, hospitality, and so on.

shero. A woman with noble and admirable qualities.

sprung. Obsessively preoccupied with another. (See *overlove.*)

tryaholic. A person who never gives up.

ultra-rageous. Beyond outrageous.

WAAWABA. Acronym for Wonderful African-American Woman with a Bright Attitude. (See *nice.*)

WAB. Abbreviation for WAAWABA.

WABometer. A very unscientific test to determine a woman's attitude toward pampering the Blackman.

woeness. Full of anxiety, misery; sorrow; lots of woe over a man.

wolf-whiffer. A chronic womanizer; a man who "gets off" on female scents. (See *dog.*)

X-er. A member of Generation X.

WORKBOOK EXERCISES

A. IF YOU WERE A . . . : THE MAN BEHIND THE MASK

You are introduced to a man who seems too good to be true. You hit it off immediately. You have so much in common. He's perfect!

But then we all have stories about a dream date turned into a nightmare. How could you have been so wrong about him? Were there signs you just ignored? Or was he a master of disguise?

Before you get into giving up your time, space, and maybe even the key to your front door, you've got to ask yourself, "Is he for real or just another plastic apple in the barrel?" Don't you deserve to know what you're in for before you take a bite?

Now here's a fun little game you can play that may reveal the man behind the mask.

With the "If You Were a . . . " game, you don't have to wait to get your heart broken. A careful survey of a Brother's answers, though given in fun, may reveal more of the man than the emperor's new clothes.

The fun part of the "If You Were a . . . " game is that it can be played anytime, anywhere—even during halftime of *Monday Night Football*.

It's not threatening, and unless *he's* read this book, he'll never suspect what you're really up to. Even if he has, there are no right or wrong answers. It's just a matter of preference. The point is, they're *your* preferences! In this game, Girlfriend, you are in control. [For a change.]

The "If You Were a . . ." game is a cross between Twenty Questions and the fill-in-the-blanks quiz you used to take in school. Now, this sample is my own subjective quiz, but feel free to use your own nouns and adjectives to reveal some surprises that may await you further down the line in your relationship:

1. If you were a dog, what kind of dog would you be? [Watch out for pit bulls and Doberman pinschers. Remember too, the more exotic the breed, the more expensive the vet bill.]

2. If you were a flower, what kind of flower would you be? [Some flowers wilt before you get them home. They are only pretty in the box.]

3. If you were a bird, what kind of bird would you be? [Do I need to warn you about vultures or buzzards?!]

4. If you were an insect, which one would you be? [Some insects nurture plants, like bees and ladybugs. Others, like mosquitoes and roaches, carry disease.]

5. If you were a spice, which spice would you be? [Your warning flag should be at full mast if he says "pepper."]

6. If you were a car, what kind of car would you be? [Show-off cars, like Benz-os and Porsches, get stolen; Caddies and Lincs hog the road. You may be better off looking for something that's sleek, safe, and economical.]

7. If you were a color, what color would you be? [Seeing red—feeling blue—turning green—acting yellow? Any of these can turn your mood to black, even if you're generally in the pink.]

8. If you were a piece of fruit, which one would you be? [If peach fuzz makes you itch, try a nectarine. One day in the sun will do a banana in. Sturdy fruit like apples and oranges are great to take on picnics. They don't squish or change colors.]

9. If you were a fabric, which fabric would you be? [Most ladies in the nineties are into natural fibers, like cotton and wool blends. Rayon and polyester are as popular as a sixties leisure suit.]

10. If you were a flavor of ice cream, what flavor would you be? [No man in his right mind will answer this one with "Tutti-Frutti." But better take a hard look at Rocky Road, Almond Fudge, and Pistachio too. There are some real nuts out there.]

11. If you were a piece of architecture, what would you be? [Dungeons and castles are a good sign that he's into domination. Gothic is cold, and ranch tells you he's a sprawler. Could your couch potato's stack of empty beer cans be far behind?]

12. If you were a cartoon character, who would you be? [Most of us have already dated a Goofy, Road Runner, Dumbo, and Mickey Mouse. I'll take Roger Rabbit over Casper the Friendly Ghost, anytime.]

13. If you were a type of cheese, which one would you be? [Swiss has holes, Muenster is smelly, and Roquefort falls apart. Your cheddars—mild, medium, and sharp, according to taste—are a good bet for being strong, flavorful, and on the practical side.]

14. If you were a character in the Bible, who would you be? [Samson was a pushover to Delilah. Some men are martyred John the Baptists or are always going through changes, like Job. Others have a king complex and you're a subject—or worse, a slave. The next time you meet a king, remember: the higher the pedestal, the greater the fall.]

15. If you were a letter in the alphabet, which one would you be? [A may mean that he's into himself. Z usually means that he'll take the last word in any dispute. I like M, as in *middle of the road* or *masculine.*]

16. If you were a wallet, what would you be made of? [The tougher the cowhide, the better the leather, I always say.]

17. If you were a musical instrument, which one would you be? [Some instruments, I don't need to tell you, are just a lot of wind. Others can bombast you with their roar. Nervous little instruments—like the flute—are hard to tune. Me? Give me a grand piano. I'm into harmony!]

18. If you were a beverage, what libation would you be? [Carbonated or noncarbonated, with or without caffeine, alcoholic or natural—those are the questions.]

19. If you were a tree, what tree would you be? [Oak trees shed their leaves in the fall. Palm trees don't have leaves, and they are nests for rats. Some trees make lousy building materials. Eucalyptus is my choice for a tree that gives shade, has utility, and sprouts leaves that can be used for medicinal purposes.]
20. If you were a fish, which fish would you be? [If he says he'd be a dolphin or a whale, you know that he doesn't know what a fish is.]

B. ARE YOU A PAMPERER?

If you've been game enough to read this manual so far, my Sister, here's a little beauty parlor game you can play with your girlfriends to find out if you are all surfing the same wave when it comes to the value you place on relationships and your feelings about the opposite sex.

[Maybe the reason you all can't hook up any male attention is because you want to go to the opera while your road-gal wants to hang out at the orgy.]

If you or your girlfriends are not into the fine noble art of pampering your relationships, you may find yourselves arguing all day. But if you are a true pamperer, only one response will be as obvious as an Alaskan oil spill.

1. It is your third date in two weeks. He's spent a fortune and you're having a wonderful time (on his dime). Now, you say, it's time to
   a. cook dinner at home (his or yours).
   b. get intimate.
   c. go on a few cheap dates for a change.
   d. do a background check on him.
2. You notice that your ex-boyfriend could be ideally suited to a new Sister you've recently met—in interests, tastes, religion, background, and so on. You will
   a. introduce them.
   b. keep them from meeting each other.
   c. let fate run its course.
   d. keep the information to yourself.
3. You're at a party. The Sisters are hugging one side of the room; the Brothers are talking sports around the bar. The music is "hot" but no one is dancing. Will you
   a. invite a Brother to dance?
   b. gravitate to the Sisters along the wall?
   c. wait to be asked to dance?
   d. go find the food?
4. Your ex-husband—the father of your two kids—hasn't given you more than a hundred dollars in a single month in the four years you've been divorced. Your seven-year-old son and four-year-old daughter adore their daddy (that triflin' SOB). Since he's always begging to see them, you can
   a. let him see them whenever he is able and pray that he gets his act together.
   b. punish him by denying him visitations.
   c. supervise the visitations.
   d. haul him back into court.
5. A young Sister on your job has excellent office skills, but out in the parking lot she's been seen making out with her boyfriend. You can
   a. become her big sister and explain business etiquette.
   b. ignore it—it's none of your business.
   c. pull her coat and tell her that it's not cool.
   d. report her activities to her immediate supervisor.

C. MATCH THIS!

Now, if you are one of those brainy Sisters who always push the class average up because you stand prepared for any test, I invite you to play "Match This!"—a game that is certain to stump those Sisters who've been sleeping through their studies.

If you've been paying any kind of attention, "Match This!" should be as easy as an open-book test.

1. She is part of the all-star audience (during sweeps week) on five or six banal television talk shows.
2. She has been dumped by every man she's slept with since 1991.
3. His white socks make him easy prey; they are a dead give-away that he'll become her incidental target.
4. The last generation of puppy lovers.
5. He's always up under some woman's dress. Even his mama says so.
6. Most likely to be engaging in cybersex.
7. People take her kindness for weakness.
8. You may not want to listen, Girlfriend, but he can shed light on any player's shady game.
9. If you can't do anything for her, you are worthless.
10. . . . live healthier than one.

a. WAAWABA
b. Baby boomers
c. Two
d. Roto-head hoochie mama
e. "Nice" guy
f. FAAWABA
g. Old O.G.
h. Dogcatcher
i. Generation X
j. Wolf-whiffer

D. THE HIMPRESSIONS RELATIONSHIP CROSS (AND UNCROSS) WORD PUZZLE

So, what's *TV Guide* doing to help you figure out your relationship? (I'll never know all the movies Ava Gardner starred in, and I can't spell *Gilligan* without some help.)

If you're into trivia but have permanently nixed more traditional crossword puzzles, here's a little mind exercise that can put you through the paces—at whatever pace you are moving.

ACROSS

1. A Sister's opinions about the Blackman.
6. Neighbor___ ; Sister___; or *Boyz 'N the* ___.
8. Obsessive longing for another.
11. If you want to go to the top in business (initials).
12. What part of ___ don't you understand?!
13. When you are totally confused, you're in a ___.
14. The miracle maker.
15. Vulgar slang for "woman with loose morals."
17. Innuendo for "sex," G-rated.
20. One who never gives up.
21. The opposite of down; bright spirits.
22. Proper form of address for all women.
23. Very cool; or, joined at the ___.
26. What makes life worth living.
27. A retro-virgin's sexual release.
31. They are the Blackman's Achilles heel. Beware!
33. A country in Europe that is loaded with potential for American Sisters (initials).
34. Someone born in the sixties.
35. Don't leave home without it.
36. Feminine for "Right on, Bro" (two words).

DOWN

1. A fast and brash FAAWABA who is exceptionally outspoken.
2. Love is only ___ in the movies.
3. Hero (female).
4. A sexual terrorist's attack.
5. Fear of using sexual protection.
6. Old-fashioned slang for Cadillac; pork.
7. Opposite of don't; or hair___.
9. ___ and behold (expression of surprise).
10. A seasoned con artist (initials).
16. The last word in kindness, from the author's point of view.
18. On-line sex.

19. A man who totally disrespects women.
24. Intended victim, or intravenous(ly) (abbreviation).
25. A FAAWABA's response to any question.
28. Obsessed with; strung out behind.
29. Start with a smile here, and it'll make your whole day.
30. Not sexually active (initials).
32. WAAWABAs (acronym).

ANSWERS TO WORKBOOK EXERCISES

B. Are You a Pamperer?: 1-a, 2-a, 3-a, 4-a, and 5-a.

C. Match This!: 1-d, 2-h, 3-e, 4-b, 5-j, 6-i, 7-a, 8-g, 9-f, and 10-c.

D. The Himpressions Relationship Cross (and Uncross) Word Puzzle:

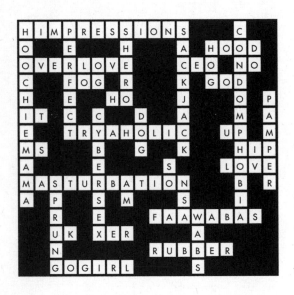

ABOUT THE AUTHOR

In the event that her first book is a hit, Valerie Shaw, author of *Himpressions: The Blackwoman's Guide to Pampering the Blackman,* is completing her autobiography entitled *Fifty Years: An Overnight Success.*

Working to become successful all of her life, Valerie Shaw has had careers in advertising, air travel, communications, calendar and book publishing, education, filmmaking, human resources, journalism, marketing, modeling, public relations, retail pharmacy, wholesale sales, and shoe repair—all before finding her niche as the author of a self-help book.

In 1966, when Shaw completed her bachelor's degree in liberal arts from the University of Southern California and married her handsome high school sweetheart, she thought that success was imminent.

With a divorce, the passing of a dozen years, a dozen careers, and a remarriage, she returned to USC for a master's degree in public relations, finishing with honors at the top of her class. She was certain that success was close at hand.

In 1980, Shaw became the first African-American woman on staff with the *Los Angeles Times'* "View" section and the founding mother of the Black Journalists' Association of Southern California. She could almost smell success.

It was not to be. Highlights of her next dozen years include another divorce, another remarriage, a child at age forty-one, a separation, single parenthood, two business failures, a dozen jobs, government assistance, and the unflinching belief that success was just around the corner.

So, putting together a small group of investors, Valerie Shaw founded a chain of high-technology shoe repair and shine salons in the heart of Hollywood and was elected to the prestigious Hollywood Chamber of Commerce board of directors.

With "Happy feet make a happy heart" as her motto and the "First Lady of Soles" as her moniker, Shaw gained exposure on

The Sally Jessy Raphael Show, various local news and public affairs programs, *The Love Connection, The Marsha Warfield Show, The Home Show,* and *The Nightly News with Tom Brokaw*—in hopes that she and her "cowboys," as she lovingly called her all-male crew, would become successful.

The only variable that Shaw hadn't considered in mapping out her path to success was her constantly changing labor force—drawn from a pool of old-school master cobblers and shine men, ex-convicts, gang members, and transients, all of whom had never before worked for a woman.

After three years, admitting another business failure, Shaw took a giant step closer to success, for in 1990 she had begun a business sidebar in promoting the art of pampering—starting with her cowboys and her customers.

Employing her skill as a journalist and social scientist, she discovered that the five hundred informal interviews and countless hours of conversations about building loving relationships had unexpectedly—less than one month after closing the doors of the once-famous shoe repair salon and its three satellite stores—resulted in a book.

In the spring of 1993, Valerie Shaw, former careerist, became a first-time self-published book author and full-time mother.

Selling over 30,000 copies of her book, *Himpressions: The Blackwoman's Guide to Pampering the Blackman,* under her own desktop publishing house, Turn the Page Productions, Shaw appeared on *The Montel Williams Show, Geraldo, The Jerry Springer Show,* and over 200 call-in and radio talk shows around the country.

Today, *Himpressions: The Blackwoman's Guide to Pampering the Blackman* has been expanded, updated, refined, and reissued by HarperCollins in the belief that this important message deserves the widest audience.

And so this time, with the publication *The Blackwoman's Guide to Pampering,* if she doesn't catch that illusive brass ring, Valerie Shaw, author, says she'll just keep trying. Just in case, she is fully prepared to continue writing more chapters for her autobiography, *Sixty Years: An Overnight Success.*